NORWEGIAN FOLK WEDDINGS

A Norway You Never Knew

NORWEGIAN FOLK WEDDINGS

A Norway You Never Knew

BOOK ONE

Odell M. Bjerkness

BIRCHPOINT PRESS

To go back to tradition is the first step forward.
— African saying

— SPECIAL THANKS —

Special thanks to my many relatives and friends in Norway who were instrumental in helping to make this work possible: Terje and Aud Byrknes from Byrknesøy i Gulen and Anne Marie and Per Gilbertson from Bagn i Valdres aided me in gathering the many details, dates and stories forming the core of this book. Also two other cousins provided relevant information: John Berg from Hønefoss, Norway and Marion Berg Balow of Minneapolis.

Others to thank are: Tor Dahl and John E. Xavier for editorial and fact-checking assistance, Pastor Kristin Sundt, John E. Xavier, Vera Olcott, Susan Tapp and Joann Bjerkness for proofing the book, Bob Dewey for suggestions, Jane Ann Nelson, Director of Library Services at Augsburg College for materials, Kaia R. Knutson for information on *bunads*, Ken Koop and Alison Dwyer from *Vesterheim* for photographs, Bill and Linda Lundborg for design, layout and graphics, David Smith for research and JoEllen Haugo for indexing.

Jeg vil gjerne få takke alle dere som har hjulpet meg med denne boken.

Odell M. Bjerkness
Richfield, Minnesota

First Edition, 2014

Copyright 2014

Odell Bjerkness

Birchpoint Press

6711 Lake Shore Drive

Suite 715

Richfield, Minnesota, 55423, USA

Telephone: 612.866.3699

Email: ojbjerkness@aol.com

Design: Bill and Linda Lundborg, Tides Edge Design, LLC

ISBN: 978-1-4951-3245-2

Printed in the United States of America.

Cover Illustration: An untitled oil painting dated 1870 by Romantic painter, Adolph Tidemand (1814-1876). National Gallery in Oslo. The bride wore a *bunad* (folk costume), a wedding crown and carried a songbook. The groom was at her side, as they walked out of the stave church. He, also,was carrying a book of Scriptures. Their parents were in the background as were others on the right including the fiddler, clarinetist, and huntsman shooting off a rifle. The driver of their carriage was on the far right.

Back Cover: Brudeferd i Sognefjorden (Wedding Procession on the Sognefjorden) by Hans Dahl (1888-1919) an oil painting on canvas in the private collection of Per Henrik Petersson.

Odell M. Bjerkness is Professor Emeritus of Concordia College, former Director and founder of The May Seminars Abroad program, and former Executive Director of the Concordia College Language Villages, Moorhead, Minnesota. He helped develop *Skogfjorden,* the nationally acclaimed Concordia College Norwegian Language Village and initiated similar programs for Swedish, Danish, Finnish, Chinese, and Japanese.

In 1982, His Majesty King Olav V of Norway awarded the prestigious *Sankt Olavs Medaljen* (The Saint Olav Medal) to Bjerkness, for his promoting and strengthening of Norwegian-American relations, especially with his work with *Skogfjorden.*

Since retirement he has taught a sequence of courses on Norway at the University of Minnesota's Osher Lifelong Learning Institute. In addition, Bjerkness initiated the *Fiskeboller Forening,* lecture/luncheon group in collaboration with the University of Minnesota's Osher Lifelong Learning Institute and *Mindekirken,* the Norwegian Lutheran Memorial Church. He organized the Edvard Grieg Society and was a founding board member of Norway House. He also helped launch the Concordia College Language Village's *Barnehage* (Children's Garden) program, a pre-school Norwegian language program for children two to five years old.

Other books written or edited by the author:

- *Three Folk Weddings and a Funeral, The Loss of Norwegian Traditions.* Book 2. (Richfield, Minnesota: Birchpoint Press, 2015).

- [Edited]: *Alt for Norge: The Resistance Movement in Norway During World War II* by Christian Klebo Skjervold II. (Richfield, Minnesota: Birchpoint Press, 2012).

- *From Odin to Jesus: Twenty-nine Studies in Oil of Historic Stave Churches in Norway.* (Edina: Birchpoint Press, 2012).

- *Images of the Valdres Valley: A Visual Tour of Norway's Historical Valley, from the Vikings to the Present Time, Illustrated by the Author.* (Edina: Birchpoint Press, 2010).

- (Co-author, with Wayne Ostlie and Paul Ostlie) *Montevideo, 1860 to 1930: Through their Eyes and in their Words.* (Edina, Minnesota: Birchpoint Press, 2011).

- *The Prince and the Nanny: The Life of Crown Prince Harald, now King of Norway, as told in Historical Context and Through the Journal of his Pediatric Nurse, Inga Berg.* (Bloomington, Minnesota: Skandisk, Inc., 2009).

- *Listen to the Voices: Marie and Olai.* (Richfield, Minnesota: Lightning Press, 2007).

Tradition is a clock that tells what time it was.

— Elbert Hubbard

Many of the illustrations in this book were chosen
because they give the reader context for wedding events and
add to the understanding of the 1800s.

A good painting, drawing, lithograph or watercolor tells
a story—it tells how a person lives, or what a place
looks like, or what was going on at that particular time.
A painting is another story apart from the text.

— TABLE OF CONTENTS —

He who works with his hands is a laborer.
He who works with his hands and his head is a craftsman.
He who works with his hands, his head, and his heart,
is an artist.

— St. Francis of Assisi

— FOREWORD —

Tidemand and Grieg: the Search for Norwegian National Symbols

After writing a constitution at Eidsvoll in 1814, Norwegians were emboldened to look for distinguishing features and symbols of Norway. They were trying to find characteristic elements of Norway's folk culture that would set apart Norway's traditions, particularly from Sweden and Denmark, as well as from other European cultures. Intellectuals, artists, politicians and the Olso *elite* started to search for those things that would help define the nation. They were impressed with the style and uniqueness of the folk arts created by rural, sharecropper farmers in Norway and especially by the *bunad* (regional folk costume), intricate *treskjærerarbeid* (wood carving), the *sponeske* (bentwood box), *skap* (cupboard with rosemaling), *stavkirke* (stave churches) and a multitude of other handmade items. Weddings were the inspiration for some of the best folk art.

Because color photographs play such an important visual role in this book together with music as the silent partner, it is worth noting especially the efforts of two artists: Adolph Tidemand (1814-1876) and Edvard Grieg (1847-1907). Both of them helped to define Norwegian folk arts as a symbol for the new nation.

Adolph Tidemand and Edvard Grieg were leaders in their fields: Tidemand for paintings of weddings and rural landscapes, and Grieg for composing music based on folk songs and dance melodies. Both were well-trained artists who studied abroad, mainly in Germany. They came back to Norway, if only briefly, attracted by the search for the identity of their "new" Norwegian nation.

Tidemand was fascinated by portrayals of the rural countryside, including the mountains, the fjords, but also with painting rural Norwegians in folk costumes at weddings and in farm settings. He did a series of paintings of women in *bunader* (folk costumes) in the areas of Luster and Sogn. Of special note is his interest in folk weddings: *Brudeferden i Hardanger* (Bridal Trip in Hardanger), *Bestemors brudekrone* (Grandmother's Bridal Crown) and *Norske Folkelivsbilleder* (a montage which is a combination of several distinct paintings put together as one large composite painting of Norwegian folk life).

In the case of Grieg, rural folk life was a welcoming sight after living abroad for a long period of time. Modern composer, Béla Bartók, said, "Grieg was one of the first to cast off the German yoke and turn to the music of his own people." Professor Finn Benestad, Norwegian specialist in the music of Grieg, said that he saw Grieg as a "nation builder." Grieg listened to oral traditions, folk tales, legends and melodies of old Norwegian farm culture. He gathered together these melodies, composing a series of pieces called *Lyriske stykker* (Lyric Pieces). Some of his well-known bridal compositions are: *Bryllupsdag på Troldhaugen* (Wedding Day at Troldhaugen), *Brudefølget drar forbi* (The Bridal Procession Passes), *Solfager og ormekongen* (Wedding Recessional March) and *Morgo ska du få gifta deg* (Tomorrow You Shall Marry Her.) In addition, Grieg wrote seven other pieces devoted to weddings and many songs on the theme of love, such as the familiar *Jeg elsker dig* (I Love You) and *Dulgt kjærlighed* (Hidden Love).

Many examples of the above works by Tidemand are found in this volume. They were executed during a time of great change in Norway, one of gradually asserting independence as a nation and one of pursuing new directions. In many ways, the transition from writing the constitution in 1814 to winning independence from Sweden in 1905 involved nine decades of painstaking work toward becoming a free and independent country. Developing an identity through folk culture became the "heart" of the new Norway. Norwegians were unanimous and proud to present this rediscovered culture to its own people and the world.

It should be mentioned that several fellow artists and near contemporaries of Tidemand were actively painting in the same mode. They included Johan Christian Claussen Dahl (1788-1857) and his son Hans Dahl (Siegwald Johannes Dahl (1827-1901). These artists used many of the same subjects as Tidemand such as wild mountain landscapes, waterfalls, country life and the fjords. Their style was similar, painting scenes as they actually appeared—using the naturalistic approach to painting. In addition to depicting men and women in their folk apparel, Hans Dahl created works of wedding processions including *Brudeferden få Sognefjord* (Wedding Procession in the Sognefjorden), showing the mid-fjord location of the bridal procession in boats; also with *Brudeferden i Sogn*, Hans Dahl portrayed a similar wedding procession but in this case, with the bride boarding the boat from the shore.

In addition to the visual and musical artists who attempted to define the image of Norway, four Norwegian writers exemplified similar efforts in literature. They were sometimes referred to as *De fire store* (The Big Four). First, Bjørnsterne Bjørnson (1832-1910) wrote five peasant novels. The first, *Synnøve Solbakken* was the most celebrated. Bjørnson received the Nobel Prize in literature in1903, an honor shared by only two other Norwegians: Knut Hamsun in 1920 and Sigrid Undset in 1928. Second, Jonas Lie (1863-1908), whose writings focused on nature and folk life, wrote *Familien paa Gilje* (The Family of Gilje). Third, Alexander Kielland (1849-1906) had a sincere affection for the less fortunate working class.

His most well known work was *Gift* (Poison), a condemnation of the Norwegian Latin School. The last of the four writers was playwright Henrik Ibsen (1828-1906), referred to as "the father of realism," the most frequently performed dramatist in the world after Shakespeare. His most famous work was the folk drama, *Peer Gynt*, with forty different scene changes accompanied by the famous incidental music composed by Edvard Grieg.

🐌Although photography was developed in France in the early 1800s by painter Louis Daguerre and later, in England by William Talbot, both scientists had their processes working by the 1840s. However, G. Eastman developed popular photography in 1889 in the U.S. when he invented the role film and a simple camera. As a result, most visual recordings of folk art from 1750 to 1860 were presented either as oil paintings, drawings or lithographs.

Topographic map of Norway, Sweden, Denmark and Finland, showing the Kjølen mountain range of over 900 miles long running down the spine of Norway, separating Norway from Sweden.

A German traveler once wrote:
There hides an artist in each Norwegian farmer.

The term "folk" is used about weddings in this book to describe both the cultural behavior of families and community and the practical and decorative arts originating among rural people or *folket*. Norwegian folk art began to be especially popular during the 1800s, when the city elite was searching for examples of specifically Norwegian rural culture in order to identify and celebrate Norwegian individuality.

The book is written primarily for an American audience, in part to explain to Norwegian-Americans and to others who are interested in Norwegian folk wedding traditions, including the colorful origins, variety and the exquisite folk art. Information furnished to that end includes maps, historical texts and over eighty paintings, drawings, photographs and lithographs. In addition, Norwegian-Americans may also use some of this information as a resource to express their heritage by incorporating Norwegian folk elements into their own wedding ceremonies or by referencing this work in family histories.

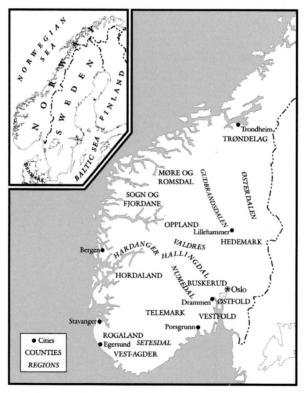

The historic areas map shows the major areas of
Norway and some of the major cities.

As with any complex social event, the folk wedding has evolved over time, changed by historical and social forces. This book explores the traditions arising from the *husmann* (tenant farmer) class in Norway. The *husmann* class is central to this discussion from several points of view: the physical environment which shaped the *husmann* life style, the influence of historical forces on the family over time, a look at their "way of life" and finally, the creation of cultural traditions and folk art objects made for and used in the wedding ceremony.

> 🐝 The use of gutt (boy) and pike (girl) in the text is based on the youthful age of many of the courting couples, but also as words of endearment and love of the family. Many times, within the family, these terms will be used well into adulthood, usually stopping after marriage.

> 🐝 Many of the reference texts used in the preparation of this book used 18th century spelling rules. The spelling of all such words has been changed, except in proper names, to use current spelling of Einar Haugen, see: *Norwegian/English Dictionary*. For example: Vågå (name of a village in Oppland); rømmegrøt (sour cream porridge and kjøgemester (master of ceremonies).

CHAPTER 1

NORWAY, ISOLATED BY GEOGRAPHY AND CLIMATE

The pre-industrial centuries in which Norwegian folk culture developed, bore little resemblance to today's increasingly urban and progressive Norway. Twenty-first century Norway has developed the technology to extract tremendous amounts of offshore oil reserves to become the wealthiest country per capita in the world. On the other hand, folk traditions were, for the most part, born in the 1700s and 1800s and nurtured in remote, small agricultural and fishing communities cut off from other parts of Norway and Europe. It was a harsh environment that shaped and, in part, led to the creation of their exquisite folk art.

To understand *husmenn* (tenant farmers) who created with their families the folklore and folk art behind folk wedding traditions, it is helpful to look at the rugged, natural environment of Norway. The environment had an effect on farmers' lives, as did the search for good land and the harsh climate. The lives of *husmenn* were very dependent on weather and economic conditions and as a result, good and bad times alternated frequently. This early period of the 1800s helped give rise to the tenant farmer's extremely frugal and difficult life and yet resulted in developing a rich folk culture found in few other countries.

🐝 A *husmann* (tenant farmer) was a person of a lower social and economic class with small rented plots of land but with the potential of life tenure of the rented farmland and buildings (*husmannsplass*) in Norway. This aspect of a Norwegian tenant's contract is special and different from any other place in Europe or Asia. In English the word could be translated many ways: sharecroppers, cotters, crofters, renters or tenant farmers. *Husmannskone* (the farmers wife) was also involved in working under the specification of the contract. *Husmann* will be used multiple times throughout the text and will not include the English translation.

🐝 *Husmenn* were guaranteed by law the same individual rights as the one who owned the land. The tenant farmer also had full jurisdiction over the farm as long as he paid the stipulated rental fee and kept the property up. Lifetime rental contracts were common but with certain exceptions. The occupant could count on his son being able to carry on after him. Eventually the daughter and sister-in-law acquired the right of such inheritance.[1]

Brudeferden i Sogn (Bridal Procession on the Sogn) by Hans Dahl, 1898. The groom helps the bride into the boat while the tapster is preparing an appetizer from a *kjenge* (an ale bowl with the traditional horse heads as handles).

Challenges to Find Good Land

All of Norway was covered with glaciers about 12,000 years ago. Only when the ice bridge between Norway and Europe began to melt and recede in 8,000 B.C.E. (Before the Common Era), did exploration begin by hunters and fishermen from the landmass of England, Denmark and Sweden. By 2,000 B.C.E. thousands of small farms began to dot the landscape, first along the southern coast and eventually all the way to Nordkapp, (North Cape), the northernmost point in Norway and Europe. Those settlers encountered the indigenous Saami or Sámi, (formerly known as Lapps) who had long since developed their coastal, reindeer herding and forest cultures. Farms joined together eventually to form small communities, and even today small farms characterize the landscape. [2]

The Norwegian fjords are long, narrow inlets of seawater reaching inland and dividing the land. In one case, the Sognefjord plunges 126 miles into the interior with great depth and steep sides. In October 21, 2009, a *National Geographic Traveler* article, "The Fjord Regions of Norway," referred to the fjords as, "the top tourist destination in the world" adding "Norway has a well-preserved rural life." [3]

A more recent article by the same magazine states: "The coast of Norway may be the most complex land edge on the planet." However, the fjords' steep sides make most of the west coast unsuitable for agriculture.

The kind of land formation so dominant in Norway is in contrast to that of neighboring Sweden, with its sloping forest reserves and farmland running along the coastline of the Bay of Bothnia all the way to Stockholm and beyond. Another interesting note is that Norway shares land borders totaling 1,592 miles with three other countries: Sweden (1,013 miles) separated by the Kjølen mountain range, Finland (457), and Russia (122). This fact has caused difficulties in dividing up individual farm plots, mineral rights, forest reserves, boundary issues and the treatment of the indigenous Saami, the Kven, Finish descendents, and other peoples.[4]

Gjende mountain lake in *Jotunheimen* (home of the giants), a mountain range in middle part of southern Norway, one of the over 450,000 fresh water lakes in Norway, most of them formed by glacial erosion.

The main and severe challenge in Norway in its early settlement period was to find rich and level land for farming. The land is rocky with over 900 miles of mountains, glaciers, and uneven terrain running down the spine of Norway and covering almost the whole countryside from north to south.

The soaring Norwegian mountain ranges have peaks
as craggy as a set of broken teeth scraping the sky.

— Tron Bach

In an almost unbelievable proportion, less than three percent of the land is suitable for agriculture. In brief, Norway is a very rock-dominated nation. The few places to find some good farmland are in the south between Kristiansand and the Oslo Fjord, around Lake Mjøsa near Lillehammer, on the west coast around the Trondheim Fjord, and in some of the major river valleys draining the east central mountainous area such as Valdres, Gudbrandsdalen, and Hallingdal.

In line with the adverse effect of fjords and mountains on agriculture, historically it has been difficult to travel within Norway due to its length and mountainous topography. A few small roads and walking paths were developed through the mountains. The *Kongesveien* (King's Highway) from Bergen to Oslo via Oppland county developed early as a path and was improved as Norwegian kings and postal authorities began to use the route. The other medieval route was the *pilegrimsleden* (pilgrimage route) from Oslo to the magnificent Gothic Nideros cathedral in Trondheim. Because of the difficult landscape, for centuries most long-distance travel in Norway was by ship.

Vøringsfossen waterfall, with a drop of over 500 feet, is located in the Måbødalen Valley at the beginning of the Hardangervidda National Park, the most visited natural attraction in Norway.

One of the defining features of Norway is its vertiginous and ever twisting roads.

— Tron Bach

The length of the mainland coastline is 15,626 miles including inlets and fjords. Adding in the distance around all the islands of the coastline, the total reaches 63,000 miles according to recent measurements by geographers recalculating the length of the coastline. The length of the coastline is remarkable considering that the distance is more than twice the number of miles around the earth's equator. In human memory, the long, circuitous, North Sea coastline with its fierce storms has posed a major challenge to travel from north to south and vice versa.

The land is also limited in space because of the shape of the country, at its widest 267 miles running east and west, a third of the distance up from the southern coast. Even more constraining is the narrow width, less than a mile across, located east and inland of the Lofoten Islands. This long shape with a wide bottom makes the profile of Norway resemble a spoon.[5]

Severe Winters Promote Indoor Work

The long, cold winter months with unfavorable weather and lack of sun have promoted work inside the home, barn or shed. The severity of changes in weather and daylight are, therefore, worth examining.

Most precipitation falls on the west coast because coastal mountain ranges draw off the moisture before it reaches the eastern side. Bergen receives 88.6 inches of precipitation a year, while inland Oslo receives only 30 inches. Much of the precipitation comes in the form of snow.

A small fishing village in the Nusfjord, Lofoton Islands, where in a good year the catch can reach nearly 75,000 long tons of prime cod. (A long ton is 2,240 pounds as opposed to a short ton of 2,000 pounds).

The interior of the country and the northern third of Norway have long, cold winters with months of darkness or reduced sunlight. The record lowest temperature is minus 60.5 degrees Fahrenheit in Finnmark, the northernmost county in Norway. The land north of the Arctic Circle covers the top third of Norway. It is in this area where summer brings the midnight sun, since daylight lasts longer in the far north.

In Tromsø, the sun shines 24 hours a day from May 20 to July 22, and even in the south it never gets completely dark at night. In the winter in the south, the sun may be up for only six or seven hours a day. Because the sun in the south is just beneath the horizon for a time each day, it produces an exotic, bluish "arctic light," while in the north, the sun in midwinter lies beneath the horizon for about two months. Thus, folk craft items such as ale bowls, wooden dippers, baskets and clothing such as the *bunad* were made indoors. Clothes, notably *bunads*, were made by hand out of wool shorn, woven and designed by the *husmennskoner* (tenants' wives).

Winter scene of a mountain cabin in the Hardangervidda mountain plateau.

Folk history is an account of events, especially in the form of a narrative, story or tale that is dealt with systematically and is important enough to be recorded.

🐦 *Stat, fylke and kommune* are the three official administrative terms used in Norway translated as state, county and municipality. Norway has 19 *fylker* and 431 *kommuner.* There is a great discrepancy in terms of the area and population of each kommune, with more than half having fewer than 5,000 people. Other non-administrative terms used include: distrikt, an unofficial area organized by common language, culture, and geographical or historical background, such as Valdres, Gudbrandsdalen, Telemark and Hallingdal. In addition, there are three church levels: the national state church which has now become as of 2012, *Det Folkekirken* (the folk church), the bispedømme (diocese), *prestegjeld* (the parish), and if there is more than one church in the *sogn*, the main church is a *sognekirke.*

Norway is divided into 19 *fylker* (administrative districts similar to counties in the U.S.) including the capital, Oslo, which is a separate county.

CHAPTER 2

FOLK HISTORY:
POLITICAL, ECONOMIC AND RELIGIOUS INFLUENCES

In addition to geography and climate, other factors of political, economic and religious nature added to Norway's isolation and are described in this chapter. Forces beyond the control of the *husmenn* shaped their lives, leading them to very difficult personal times of poverty and despair.

Much of the history of the peasant class in Norway is inextricably tied to the politics and economics of the land. The nearly two hundred-year period from 1130 to 1319 was a time of great population growth, triggering the clearing of wilderness for new farms, especially in eastern Norway. Since the king could tax cleared farmland, many farmers rented out their land rather than farm it themselves. Thus, farmers became tenants of the king, paid taxes on the rent and retained their civil status as free men.

🐝 In the late Middle Ages around 1536, Norway had between 60,000 to 70,000 farms.

From 1349 to 1351, the Black Death (the Bubonic Plague) decimated the population of Norway, particularly the remote eastern part, with a great and destructive effect on the economy. Airborne microbes and fleas from infected rats carried the disease that attacked the lymph glands in the armpits and groins of individuals. A large number of independent land-owning farmers died, as well as sharecroppers, and much agricultural production was lost. Of course, such a decline in the number of farmers meant a loss of tax revenue to the church and king.[5]

The aristocracy itself was at risk from the Black Death. However, by the 1400s, the aristocratic survivors actually benefited from the Black Death because, proportionally, with fewer people, their diet improved when more animal protein per capita was available in the form of meat, eggs and cheese. Furthermore, by the 1500s, the aristocratic state church, ever interested in power and wealth, became the largest landowner under the king, acquiring nearly one half of the land in Norway.

Political Isolation

The era from 1523 to 1905 is often referred to negatively by Norwegians as the "four-hundred year's night." The reason for this expression was that Norway was ruled first by Danish and then Swedish kings. The so-called union with Danish kings held sway from 1380 to 1814, followed by union under Swedish rulers from 1814 to 1905. The lack of leadership on both the local and national level isolated the country for centuries, with minimal interchange with the rest of Europe. As a result, Norway had little self-identity or influence locally, nationally or internationally, except through the Danish and Swedish monarchies located in Copenhagen and Stockholm and through some associations with the Hanseatic League.[6]

❧ The following four wedding paintings were found on the inside of a bridal trunk from the 1800s. In the trunk was a letter dated 1832, belonging to Hoeg in Sør-Trøndelag, explaining the paintings on the four panels. Ole Andersen from Skaun, Sør-Trøndelag was probably the painter judging by the similar handwriting on the letter and the lettering on the trunk. *Stabbedansen* (stump dancing) was a traditional activity at the close of a wedding party. All the guests would take a turn as a couple, dancing on the stump. Not everyone wanted to stand on the stump in public.

In the upper left are the bride and groom in front of a *beining* (money bowl) filled with gifts, and on their left are two clergy. In the middle, is a man holding a *kaggehammer* (keg hammer) to open the keg of beer, another putting money in the bowl and a third handing a mug of beer to another guest.

This panel pictures a man holding a lamb while three other men are carrying in the large cooking kettle. Note the men all wearing red pointed hats, knickerbockers and long stockings and the women wearing simple regional bunader of that period.

At the beginning of the 1600s and on, Norway played a minor role in the two most important European movements of that time: the Renaissance and the Industrial Revolution. The *husmenn* were on the lowest end of the economic scale, and suffered the most during this era. Foreign rulers confiscated the best land, raised taxes on the farmers and dominated trade. Throughout this period, kings were often traveling around the country on military or court concerns but, most importantly, to collect taxes in the form of farm produce. The Danish nobility held the best positions in Norway, and written Norwegian was forever altered as Danish spelling was superimposed on written Norwegian by the educated élites. Traditional spoken Norwegian persisted mainly in regional or local dialects.

The 1600s and 1700s continued to be difficult times for *husmenn* as a result of hunger and disease. A high birth rate was negated by a similarly high infant mortality rate. Unhealthy living conditions prevailed, for houses were drafty and dirty, featuring

hearths in the middle of open rooms too inefficient for smoke to escape through an opening in the ceiling. As rooms were full of smoke and soot, respiratory diseases were common. To keep up the appearances of the home, repeated coats of whitewash were applied to the walls and ceilings. One positive development was in land acquisition opportunities, in that some sharecroppers and farmer-owners received permission to buy land from the crown and nobility who needed to raise money to pay for preparations for chronically recurring wars and for their costly lifestyles.

The Norwegian "stump dance" with a couple dancing on the narrow, round stump of a tree, "better to get to know you," while other couples wait in line as two fiddlers play on.

By the 1800s some farmers owned their land, mostly in small plots. Because so little land was available in the first place during this time, an increasing number of poor were allowed to farm a small portion of the owners' land in exchange for cash rent and working for the owners. Often children of *husmenn* became servants or hired men or women working for room, board and sometimes even clothing.

Break-up of farms rarely occurred because the traditional inheritance practice of *odelsrett* (rights of the oldest). If the land were owned, the oldest male son inherited everything including

A couple is dancing while another woman is attempting to cut in. Two bored men are sitting at a table playing cards.

the land, animals, buildings and their contents. If there were no sons, the oldest daughter was the sole beneficiary and she became a very desirable bride. Younger sons who wished to farm could opt to become *husmenn*, working small pieces of land with one-room cottages for their families and a few outbuildings. Much later, in 1974, *odelsloven* (elder's law) was changed so that males and females now have equal inheritance rights in order of date of birth.

Norwegian identity grew gradually, and by the end of the Napoleonic Wars (1799-1815), Norwegians started to think of building a nation. These wars pitted France against a shifting alliance of European powers. Denmark was on the wrong side near the end of the main conflict (before Waterloo) and had to cede Norway to Sweden. It was in 1814 that the Norwegian constitution was signed at Eidsvoll. After a brief war with Sweden, King Karl Johan III of Sweden agreed to a proposed union with a shared king. In that context, Sweden retained its role in directing Norwegian foreign affairs and kept that status until Norwegian independence in 1905.

Due to such a long period of more than four centuries under foreign domination, Norwegians began to ask the question that continues to our time: What are the basic elements of Norway's character? Since only 25 percent of the people lived in cities in 1825, many people believed that true Norwegian character was found in the countryside and in rural folk culture. Yet, because of general uncertainty and the major factor of ongoing poverty, in the 1850s people began to think about leaving Norway and indeed many did, as was the case in Ireland. In 1920, fifteen years after independence, the urban population had grown to 45 percent of the Norwegian people. The urbanization trend continues in Norway today, and the rural versus urban discussions continue.[7]

An early wedding painting in Gol, Hallingdal in 1699 of a very wealthy farmer, Bjørn Frøsaak, with his newest wife on his right and his other wife on the left, surrounded by his sons and daughters.

Influence of the Christian Church

Many traditional symbols help define Norway, but the wooden stave churches are among the most significant. Today they are more than just regional structures; they are national and international treasures. Moreover, stave churches are Norway's unique contribution to world architecture.

The farmer class in Norway became closely connected to the church when Christianity was introduced to Norway first by King Olav I Trygvasson in the years 995-1000 C.E. and secondly in 1015-1028 C.E. by King Olav II Haraldson. *Husmenn* grew up on farms around the church, went to its services, were members of the parish, and built and repaired the buildings. They carved intricate designs on the walls, portals, posts, and altarpieces. These wooden carvings remain among the best examples of European medieval art. Two carvings found in almost all stave churches are in the forms of a dragon or evil spirit masks and a Christian cross, indicative of the struggle and juxtaposition between Norse native traditions and the then, new and strange, Christian innovations. Design ideas were also taken from churches, copied onto storage buildings, barns, granaries and farmhouses. Obviously, these contacts with the Christian (Roman Catholic) Church had a great influence on all aspects of people's lives and, particularly, on the folk arts.

Art specialists estimate that a range of from 1,000 to 2,000 rural, wooden stave churches once stood all over Norway up to the year 1537. Over the centuries many burned down or were dismantled or were modified due to the growth of the congregation. Many churches were located in remote, mountainous areas of south-central Norway. Twenty-eight stave churches still remain, over half of them in three counties: nine in Oppland, five in Buskerud and four in Sogn og Fjordane. Some of the richest folk art in Norway came from these three counties.

Then as now, food and mealtimes played a central role in early 1700s farm folk weddings. This painting on a wooden panel is from 1718, made in Østfold. Inspired by the Biblical wedding in Cana, the artist superimposes the Norwegian wedding party into the context of this Biblical wedding. The top of first panel finds Jesus on the right, the one with a halo, near to both groom on left, and bride on his right. The second panel shows the musicians starting on the left, playing the violin, clarinet, horn, with a group of percussionists and bell ringers on far right. The lower panel depicts the six vessels of water to be turned into wine. Credit: Norsk Folkemuseum in Oslo.

Farmer/craftsmen built stave churches using methods akin to the modern pre-fabrication. In other words, the various parts were pre-cut, labeled and then placed in their appropriate places. Not including roofing shingles, the largest churches had over 2,000 parts. It is likely that similar construction methods were used in all the stave churches, but with modification based on regional styles of rosemaling and carving. The secret ingredient for the preservation of the wooden logs in stave churches was pine tar, made from the resin of pine trees.[8]

The Reinli stave church was built in 1326. The Parish Pastor Thomas Barth and his congregation assembled in front of the church in 1890. That same year, Barth also married Marit and Martin Dolvesknatten in the Bagn village church in Sør-Aurdal, Valdres.

The Reinli Stave Church

The Reinli stave church in Oppland county, could serve, in general, as a model of the other 27 stave churches still standing in Norway. Early in the 1300s and located high above the Begna river, the Reinli *Stavkirke* was the third religious site in succession to have risen on this mountaintop. Long before the Renili church was built in the 1300s, two former *Heithinh hov* (pagan temples) were located there. Before the eleventh-century Christianization of the Valdres valley, pagan groups worshipped and burned sacrifices in honor of their gods. Archaeologists have verified the existence of these pagan altars through excavations of the site and discovery of artifacts from this era such as charred animal bones.

Lying in the valley below the Reinli stave church, the little village of Bagn was surrounded by a cluster of centuries-old farms. The farms took many of their names from the formation of the land (*berg* meaning hill) and Norwegians took their names from names of farms where they worked or lived. In some cases, farmers used their occupations as a last name: i.e. Martin *Hjulmaker*, Martin the wheelwright. Most farms in the area were divided into sub-farms for *husmenn*, with life tenure on the farm. It was a poor man's life, and when conditions became intolerable, sharecroppers looked for other options. Such was the case in Valdres: of all regions in Norway in the 1800s, Valdres led in per capita emigration to the United States.

Painting by the village pastor, Niels Hedaberg, of a wedding meal in Vinsarvik, Hordaland, about 1820. The bridal couple is at the end on the high bench to the left, with relatives all around. It was a rowdy group, with men in the middle fighting, and on the far right a man dancing, with his foot tipping over his bowl of food as it was being delivered.

The *kjøkemester* (master of ceremonies) holding a "keg hammer" to tap the ale barrel while the people eagerly await that moment, featuring a violin player on the right and in the center bottom, a squabble between a cat and a dog.

Notions of Evil

From the Viking age (793-1066) and on, pagan gods such as *Odin* (principal Norse god and god of war), *Thor* (son of Odin and god of thunder) and *Freya* (goddess of love and fertility) were believed to protect people from evil spirits. People communicated with these gods through vows and rituals. Names of some of the gods have survived, preserved in English as names of persons or of days of the week: *Tyr* for Tuesday, *Odin* for Wednesday, *Thor* for Thursday and *Freya* for Friday. Although the Roman Catholic Church in the 1100s introduced Jesus as the main replacement for pagan gods, the Norwegian people were not sure whether they could completely abandon their old gods. The result is seen in stave churches with multiple dragonheads and pagan masks next to Christian crosses. Pagan symbols were kept to frighten away evil spirits and as a backup in case Christian symbols failed. Gradually, Christian symbols began to dominate, necessitating the creation of new and different types of pagan icons.

🐝 A wide variety of jewelry was worn with folk dresses. There were many superstitions linked to silver jewelry. For instance, a small brooch was always pinned to the shirt of a newborn child to protect it from creatures from the nether world.

It took many hundreds of years before people were willing to give up their old beliefs in hidden spirits. After pagan gods began to disappear, different figures began to emerge such as *trolls* reputed to be of great strength, huge, messy giants with large and long, running noses They had only one eye, large mouths and long bushy tails, living in the forests and mountains. They were a bit stupid and could be outsmarted by clever men. *The hulder*

The giant troll in *Gimle* (it is called the dining room at Skogfjorden, the Norwegian Language Village but in Norse mythology, it is the golden hall where gods live after the end of the world). This painting was the work of another well-established rosemaler, Nils Ellingsgard. The troll is called *Dovre gubben*, the king of all trolls, who lives in the Dovre Mountains.

(an enticing woman figure), beautiful in appearance but with long cow-like tails, were said to inhabit the forested hills and to cast spells on Christian men. If they married, their tails fell off. *Nisse* were portrayed as short, pudgy, farm-dwelling pixies, wearing grey clothes and red pointed stocking caps. They were the first farmers who cleared the land and also were known as farmers from the burial mounds. Their main duty was to watch over the farm and to see that the animals were well cared for. Other creatures included *draugen*, protector of those who died at sea, and the river sprite, *nøkken*. Some of these new entrants could also be protectors if well treated. Nevertheless, in the minds of many people, evil spirits could still cause death, storms, floods or the death of a child by drowning.[9]

Sigmund Aarseth painted the three troll-chefs with their noses in the soup. Its morale is "too many cooks in the kitchen spoil the broth." The humorous painting graces the wall beside the kitchen door at *Skogfjorden*.

🐝 People believed in a Christian God and Jesus who would stand between them and evil forces. Their Christian faith had become their protector against evil. Faith brought them guidance to deal with their family and neighbors and to handle suffering, disaster and death.

🐝 The fear of evil spirits can be seen in the context of folk weddings. A bride was believed by many to be especially vulnerable to the magic of evil beings. She was guarded well and precautions were made to protect her. Some examples include slamming the door of the wedding party room three times. Rifle shots could be fired over the bride's head on the way to church. Shooting and noisemakers are, even today, reminiscent of attempts to scare away evil spirits and make it widely known that a wedding is a happy event. The modern practice of tying cans on the back of the newly married couple's car stems from this old practice of scaring off evil spirits and calling attention to the marriage celebration. Throwing rice on the married couple is another example of blessing the bride and groom as they leave the church, frightening away evil spirits.

The Hulder [Huldra at Norwegian Village] (femme fatale) inhabits hills and mountains, but beware, she is a wicked, alluring siren. She is beautiful in appearance but with a long, cow-like tail sticking out of her dress. According to legend, when she marries, her tail falls off. Painted by renowned rosemaler, Sigmund Aarseth, at *Skogfjorden,* the Concordia College Norwegian Language Village in Bemidji, Minnesota.

Church Membership and Marriage

After the Reformation in 1537, it is not surprising to note increasing pressure on the bride and groom to be baptized and confirmed in the Christian faith in the Lutheran State Church. In Norway, the Reformation evolved from reform to wholesale replacement of the Roman Catholic Church and resulted in the establishment of the Lutheran State Church of Norway. That church required young people to learn the fundamentals of Christianity and of the Bible: the Ten Commandments, the Lord's Prayer, Luther's Small Catechism and prayers for both morning and evening worship. In addition, the confirmands at about the age of fourteen had to declare their faith publicly and make this commitment standing in front of the congregation. Only then were they considered adults and old enough to be married.

A further church obligation, was that after the marriage and wedding date were agreed upon, the banns announcing the name of the bride were read aloud at a regular Sunday service for three Sundays in a row. (Some Lutheran churches both in Norway and the U.S. still practice this custom.) The purpose of these banns was to make it possible for members to come forward to protest the marriage. Such protest is rarely expressed in the U.S. today but in the 1800s in Norway, survival of a couple depended on avoiding problems before marriage. Such problems included verifying that the potential groom was not a criminal, a deserter from the army, in debt or had any other serious problems that could prevent a successful marriage. In addition, the law forbade marriage between cousins and second cousins, and three weeks would give enough time for any blood relationship of the bride and groom to be verified.

"Brudeferden i Hardanger" (Wedding boat trip in Hardanger) is an 1848 painting by Adolph Tidemand. He painted the details of the people and Hans Gude furnished the background. The bride sits astern (the back) with the groom; the violinist is at the bow (front); the hunter is shooting off his gun to chase away evil spirits, while the *kjellermann* (tapster) serves ale to the party.

Need for Marriage

During all these pre- and post- Black Death periods (1349-1351) discussed above, marriage was a revered relationship in Norway because men like Jon, Martin and Olai (these three men were the husbands in the three weddings discussed in Book Two of this trilogy titled *Three Folk Weddings and Funeral, The Loss of Norwegian Traditions*) needed wives not only to bear children, but also for family help on the farm and ultimately to help provide a place for the parents and parents-in-law to retire.

The tasks of the wife were legendary and the list long of their obligations. First in the house: care of the children, preparation of five meals a day, including snacks and lunches; churning butter, making cheese, brewing beer, spinning yarn, weaving blankets, washing clothes outside, fueling a wood-burning stove to heat water and sewing clothes for the family. Likewise, the list of women's outside work was similarly lengthy: milking cows and goats was clearly in the domain of women, as was shearing sheep; feeding animals; gathering, chopping, and sawing wood, all the while tending to stoves both for cooking and heating. Wood-burning stoves took an immense amount of time because of the constant care and need for dry, split wood. In sum, the time to do the "chores" took all of the wife's waking hours, usually using only simple cookware, an open fire and primitive tools. Yet, this was the economics of the home, the basis for the *husmann's* existence.

Based on a Norwegian fairy tale, *The Troll and the Princess* was depicted by Sigmund Aarseth at *Skogfjorden.*

Children Out of Wedlock

As noted earlier, while young Norwegians were subject to social rules, they could still meet in ways that would lead to close relationships. Even among religious people and the upper class, a certain level of promiscuity was common behavior. However, the attitude of rural people toward illegitimate birth did vary from one place to another. The Norwegian sociologist, Eilert Lund Sundt, pointed out in his study that in the Sogn area in 1851, 73 percent of couples had children out of wedlock. In another area, Sunnfjord, a district in Sogn og Fjordane county, the rate was 21 percent, so the percentage did vary by area. In general, it was not unusual for couples to have one or two children before they married. As in today's Norway, in Sundt's time no civil laws forbade young people from living together. In the summer, casual sleeping arrangements known as *hattefriing* had young women of marriageable age sleeping in barns, *stabbur* (storage buildings) and other outbuildings, which were said to be because of overcrowding in the main house. Such arrangements along with the indifference of the community, led to many illegitimate births.[10]

Sigmund Araseth spent a week at the Norwegian Village in 1976, rosemaling the entire ceiling and walls of the dining room. A day was spent mixing American paint tones to match colors he used in Norway. He climbed tall ladders and scaffolding, lying on his back painting with six-inch brushes. Look for the one smiling face on the Acanthus flowers.

Money and Alcohol Abuse

People during this post-Black Death period, put a lot of money into traditional wedding events as they do today. Often the celebration lasted three to four days and sometimes even five days or longer. The number of guests would depend on the wealth of the family and what they thought others in the community expected of them.

Government officials were concerned about the great amount of money spent on weddings by those who could ill afford it, at which point the county might have to step in with its resources to help them. Another issue was the amount of alcohol consumed by the guests. For example, a local ordinance passed in Vågå in Gulbrandsdalen in 1815 made this point:

> It is recognized how damaging and expensive the large weddings and wakes are and how large amounts of grain supplies are consumed with no benefit. This unwholesome custom shall be restricted with the following ordinance. No one in the future shall use more than a maximum of 20 quarts of distilled spirits and no more beer than can be contained in one barrel of malt in any wedding or wake. The gatherings shall not last longer than the evening of the second day, except for some of the nearest relatives, who may remain over the second night. The ordinance of January 20, 1785 already forbids use of coffee or punch at such gatherings.

Fanatitere (Religious Zealot) portraying a fire and brimstone sermon, with mortified listeners cringing in fear. An 1866 oil painting by A. Tidemand, now in *Nationalmuseum* in Stockholm,

If anyone is found to use more beer or distilled spirits than permitted by this rule, they shall pay a fine of 40 *riksdalere* (state dollars) half given to the poor of the parish and half to the informer. Guests shall be told at the time of the invitation how long they can stay at the wedding. To avoid abuse the host shall be required to show to a responsible person all the supplies of drink which are set aside for the guests so that this person may be witness to the truth in case of an accusation.[11] Records do not indicate if anyone ever paid the 40-riksdaler fine (roughly $4,000 in 2014) in Vågå but three- and five-day weddings continued well into the 1900s, with the size and duration of the weddings based on the family's financial condition, not on the ordinance.

Ale bowl with rosemaling

Ten or twelve barrels of ale might have been brewed for a wedding. Strong or stout ale (a heavy dark brown brew like porter's ale which is also a dark beer resembling light stout but made from charred or browned malt) gave the impression that the family was prosperous and their holdings well managed. After the wedding ceremony, friends and family went to a reception at the newlywed's new home or at the bride's house. Ale bowls were soon empty at the reception and guests and family would throw coins into the bowls that they drank out of. At some point the bride was expected to throw a small bowl over the roof of her new home. If the bowl did not make it over the roof, the superstition was that she could expect bad luck in the future.[20]

A *kjenge* (turned ale bowl) with crowned lion and serpent head handles, painted by Thomas Luraas in 1845. The text around the lip of the bowl reads "God give us peace and good harvest, then, we take many good drinks from me." The lion may represent courage and joy while the serpent holds the food of temptation.

The bridal party has to make a long trip from the farm to the church as seen between the trees in the background, left. An 1875 painting by Adolph Tidemand, *"Bridal Party Trip across the Lake."* Rasmus Meyer's Collection, Bergen.

CHAPTER 3
NINETEENTH CENTURY INFLUENCE ON LOCAL COMMUNITY

To understand the social influences on tenant farmers and the development of their folk art, it is helpful to look at their way of life and folklore in the 1800s, i.e. the consistent and integrated way of life of both the individual and groups, as typified by their social class, manners, attitudes and possessions.

Class Consciousness

Norway in the 1800s was a very class-conscious society, with *bønder* (farmers), *husmenn* (sharecroppers) and *arbeidere* (laborers) forming the lowest, most populous class. It is important to note that all three were called farmers in the broad sense of the term but with real social and economic differences. A great distinction existed between *bønder* and the other two because *bønder* were the ones who owned land and in some cases were even from the upper classes. Large landowners, small-scale businessmen, educated people, such as teachers and pastors, high-level clerical workers—all were the middle class.

The upper class was drawn from those who inherited great wealth, the wealthy businessmen, high government officials and representatives of the Danish or Swedish monarchy. Yet, members of the foreign ruling nobility were not a very visible factor during their reigns over Norway, because the Danes governed from Copenhagen from 1536–1814, while the Swedes carried on in like fashion from Stockholm from 1814-1905.

The farmer-owners managed small plots, maybe 5 to 25 acres, whereas the *husmann* farmed only an acre or two of his land but could also lease and work more land on a sharecropper basis. The *husmann* could get permission to build a small house and barn for animals, working off the rent by giving the owner some of his crop and helping the owner with his chores. The lowest class, *arbeider klasse,* was the farmer-laborer who worked on the farm for room and board and a small wage.

Of the numerically dominant agricultural sector, *husmann* had to sign a contract. In 1816 Ole Eiversen of Hallingdal (an extended valley running through the northern

Fanitullen (rascal) of a young man surreptitiously tapping the keg of ale in the hotel cellar, painted in oil by A. Tidemand in 1853 at Sanderstølen Hotel.

and eastern part of Buskerud county), in 1816, signed such a contract, in part, reading:

> Ole Eiverson, including his wife, has to be obligated to work for me at all times of the year and has to be willing to come to work after I have given them the least calling, either it is to work in the spring's work, the summer, the fall and the winter work and at all times which, I, the owner, will need them: and they have to be polite and reliable in that work that they are put to do.[11]

Farmers and persons of the educated class were strongly forbidden by their families to intermarry. Although they lived in the same country, they lived in a totally different culture and social world. Most important, marriage was, as it often is today, an economic institution. Young people looked for a partner who, by marriage, could increase their own social and economic status.

Norwegian farmers, in contrast to some Europeans, could read and write, due to the requirement of the Lutheran State Church that the catechism be read and studied by all church members. The farmers could express themselves well, although books other than the Bible and children's schoolbooks were not found in great numbers in many households. To their great credit, beyond book knowledge, the *husmann* class and their families knew how to subsist in, sometimes, difficult environments. They knew how to plant, harvest crops and raise cows,

Portreittstudie: Bonde fra Vossevangen
(Portrait study in oil of a farmer from
Vossevangen) by A. Tidemand.

pigs and goats, and to prevail over their circumstances.

Norwegian farmers had a season-based plan: plant in the spring, harvest in the fall and use the *jordkjeller* (root cellar) to preserve food for seven or eight months during the winter, including root plants such as potatoes, rutabagas, turnips, beets and carrots. They also had the reputation of being good neighbors, a trait that they brought to Minnesota, among other places, known as "Minnesota nice." *Husmenn* had a reputation for helping others in need and creating a friendly community.

The basic unit of production was the family or household. Families consumed what they produced, although a portion of their output could be sold or paid to the landlord as rent. Productivity per worker and yield per unit of land was unusually low. The class structure of an agrarian Norway has tended to disappear as society industrialized. Some aspects of the farmer-based social and cultural models persisted under later economic regimes, thus becoming a great source of folk traditions. The *husmann* class, as the majority of the Norwegian population, accounted for the bulk of the people who left for America in the mid-1800s and early 1900s. As was mentioned earlier, the Valdres region was a prime example of a place of mass emigration.

Her mother shows off the *bryllupkrone* (bridal crown) to her daughter in anticipation of the daughter's wedding. "Ung elsk," (young love), painting by Nils Berslien, 1800s.

Women's Rights and Dowries

In contemporary Norwegian society, marriage is between two individuals based on their preference for each other. Individual couples are in charge of their lives and they have few responsibilities to anyone other than their closest family. In contrast, marriage customs in the 1800s in Norway were for a different society, where the structure was based on *ætt* (the family), not the individual. The family not only included the blood relatives but also a psychological bond with ancestors. A marriage was a matter for the couple involved and their respective families.

In the early 1800s, marriage was a civil contract, although the ceremony took place in church where banns were announced. Various social gestures were included in the marriage process. The groom offered the bride a wedding gift to compensate for the family's loss of a member. The bride's family gave her a dowry that matched the gift from the groom. These gifts could be related to both household and farm, i.e., personal items such as livestock, land, furniture and kitchenware.

A young boy with a *lur* (trumpet-like wooden shepherd's horn similar to an alpenhorn) on his back and a red hat on his head proposes to an attractive girl carrying a basket. Both are wearing *bunader* in this 1857 painting by Adolph Tidemand.

All of those items became the bride's personal property and could be quite valuable. Since large gifts like land were often at stake, marriage was clearly a serious family matter. The size of these gifts depended on the social and economic status of their families and, in some cases, negotiating could be quite complex. Since the ownership of land was limited and expensive, women were brought up to accept their father's choice of a mate; however, it was common for a father to seek the consent of a daughter.

The European way of looking at the idea of romance through the French songs of the troubadours was not accepted in 1800s Norway. Samuel Laing points out that the English expression "true love" is not derived from the sentimental word, "love," or from the fidelity of the lover nor from the Scandinavian synonym to *amor*. Rather, "true love" arises from the synonym *lex* or law or *lov,* in Norwegian. The Norwegian word *trolov* meant true love, originally, but contracted or pledged under the law. A man might be a "true lover," i.e., in debt for ten *kroner*, as well as in love with his sweetheart.[12]

The Norse system was largely patriarchal, but the rights of women were more advanced than in other countries. As mentioned above, a woman could own property. If she decided to divorce her husband, she kept both the farmhouse and the land. Even in earlier Viking times, women could present their reasons for divorce by pleading their case before the king at a *ting* (later the *ting* became a legislative and judicial assembly of free men in Norway). The king would convene an annual gathering so that people, including women, could vent their concerns. This right of addressing the king, gave women power. A woman could choose to start wearing trousers, indicating there was trouble between the couple and divorce was imminent. Hence, the question arose of, "who is wearing the pants in a family."[12]

Adolph Tidemand used as a model for the painting, *Ingeborg Andresdatter Gulsvig* from Hallingdal. She was 17 years old and was to marry a 20-year-old *lensmann* (sheriff) on June 16, 1849. Tidemand was a guest at the wedding.

Another form of power was the ownership of the key to the chest where the family's valuables were stored. Often, men would leave for a period of time—in the Viking period this could be for three or four months. In such a case, the wife was given the key for safekeeping and when the spouse returned she did not always give the key back. Another view is that the women kept the keys all the time. In the aftermath of divorce or death of the husband, a widow as owner of property could marry again without the consent of her father or anyone else. Boys and girls were usually considered young adults after confirmation at the age of 14 or 15.

Attitude Toward Marriage

Contrary to the standing joke of the Norwegian bachelor farmer, most people in Norway did marry. By the end of the 1800s, a marriage was for life and was rarely broken except by death. Life without a spouse was difficult; when a death occurred, it was usual for the survivor to find another mate. In the case of Marit Berg's death at the age of 42 in 1907, after she bore eight children, Martin Berg never did re-marry. He lived alone the rest of his 17 years, dying at 65 in 1925 in Bagn.

The *bedemann* (intermediary) is making the case for marriage for the girl's suitor. The father and mother look on skeptically. Lithograph, from an 1861 painting by A. Schioll.

Selecting a Mate

In the 1800s, selecting a spouse followed a number of protocols in which social class and economic conditions played important roles. Most of the time, mates were chosen from people in the local community and parish. Decisions in choosing a partner were influenced by parents but most of the time, couples made their own decisions. They met their neighbors informally, and made friends with others in school, church at weddings, funerals, social gatherings or temperance meetings. Dances, a good opportunity to socialize, were usually held on special occasions such as harvest festivals or barn raisings.

"Look up at the Maiden" is a 1905 lithograph by Th. Kittelson, and an example of *nattefrieri* (night visiting). The young man is looking up at the girl peeking out of a window of a *stabbur* (storage building).

Other places where relationships flourished were on mountain farms or in cabins. Many adolescent girls spent much of the summer at the family's *seter* (mountain farm) tending cows and goats and making butter and cheese. Young friends who worked on nearby family farms would come to visit them at the farm. Rules were enforced in varying degrees for this kind of courting. The visit could only be on a weeknight, not on Saturday or Sunday. If things went well, eventually, a *beleman* (intermediary) would return with the suitor and the suitor would have to explain to her parents his economic, and social situation for marriage.

Another method of meeting was "night courting" where boys would visit the girl in her home at night in groups or sometimes alone. If the girl were expecting a visit, she would lie in her bed fully clothed. The outside door would be conveniently left unlocked. Another term used for this method was "bundling" or *natteløper* (night roaming).

Bundling was a widely accepted practice in colonial America and even among religious conservative groups in Norway like the Haugeans. They were followers of Hans Nielsen Hauge (1771-1824) who was an itinerant preacher who championed a religious awakening in Norway; he also was a major force in forbidding ordained preachers in the pulpit. These bundling ways of informal meeting were just about the only way young people could get to know one another since at most formal or social situations like church or parties, the boys and girls did not sit together, boys on the right, girls on the left.

Jingling and Scattering

After a couple had been together, possibly courting for a period of time, their friends would start to tease them when they were seen holding hands or sitting alone together. This teasing custom was called "jingling" and involved putting stones in containers or using cowbells to disturb the couple. If the couple did not get married after being "jingled" or "belled," they would feel ashamed and embarrassed for waiting too long for the proposal to come. Another custom in the Sogn area was called "scattering." Friends would make a line of sawdust from the girl's house to her boyfriend's home to show that everybody knew of the relationship.

Pleadings for a Mate

The desire to meet eligible young people of the opposite sex was strong, sometimes fanciful, and often based on superstition. For example, they could engage in some of the following: if you could twist the flower of a bluebell from its stem without tearing it, you could get your true love. Another more drastic tactic was to cut your little finger, put some of the blood on an apple and offer it to the love of your life hoping he or she would eat the apple. Even prayers from Østfold (area on east side of Oslofjord) were used to help find the "right one."

> Think about me, O God,
> And about all maidens,
> And let me
> by your great mercy
> Be called to the bridal bed.
> Get me a man tall,
> handsome and slender
> Amen

Another plea was spoken out loud when curtsying to the first new moon of the year:

> Good evening new moon.
> Welcome to our town.
> Tell me, whose table shall I spread?
> Whose bed shall I red?
> Which man shall I own? [13]

Brudekrona (Bridal crown) is being fitted for the bride-to-be with grandmother and bride's sister looking on. Adolph Tidemand signed his name and the date, 1870, in lower right corner of the family trunk.

Marriage Proposal

As was mentioned before, a formal engagement proposal sometimes was made through an intermediary, a *bedemann* or wooing man. He would contact the girl's father on behalf of the boy's father. His visit would be on a Saturday afternoon,

Fjøsfrieri (Cow barn) with the little brother lying in the loft at the top center peeking at the embracing young couple. 1904 painting by Nikolai Astrup.

with Saturdays before Christmas and Easter considered the most propitious time for a reply. If the first visit were positive, the intermediary and the young man would have to explain his economic fitness to be married. If there was an agreement, a verbal engagement was made which obligated both girl and man to a wedding ceremony. According to the law, it was a legal contract. If a child was born before the wedding ceremony, the future marriage made the child legitimate.

Man With Many Mangle Boards

A *mangletre* (mangle board) is a flat board with a handle, usually elaborately carved and used to smooth and press linen, and was employed in the 1800s for ironing clothing until the flatiron was invented. A mangle consisted of a flat board, about two feet long and four inches wide made from a fir tree. A raised handle was at one end and sometimes an additional handle or knob was at the other end. The underside of the mangle board was completely smooth. A dampened piece of linen cloth was wound around the accompanying large dowel, and rolled back and forth using the mangle board.

A mangle board was considered an essential item for all newly married housewives, as well as a piece of art. The sometimes elaborately carved, dated, signed and painted *mangletre* would earn the attention of a potential bride. The motifs on the board could be scrolls, birds, geometric figures or floral designs. A suitor would carve one for his girlfriend and leave it at her door. If she took it into the house, his mangle was accepted as a proposal. If it was left at the door, his proposal was turned down. The suitor could not use the same board a second time, so he would make another and perhaps another. A Norwegian folk saying warns: "Beware of the suitor with many mangle boards." He may have proposed to, and then been rejected by many women.

The *mangletre* (mangle board) with horse-shaped handles for working wrinkles out of cloth, used with a short, thick, round dowel. It was given as a betrothal gift and featured numerous and varied designs.

Linked Wooden Spoons Connected by a Wooden Chain

Another similar symbol of courting was the *skjeer* (wooden spoons), with a wooden chain carved from one block. Spoons in Norway are symbols of love. When a young man went to court a young woman, they would desire some private time. In Norway it was often too cold to sit outside, so an unheated room was provided for the young couple to become acquainted. The father of the girl, aware of the possibilities of the situation, required that the suitor keep his hands working on some task like carving two spoons and a chain. By requiring a certain amount of work to be done by the end of each visit, the father was somewhat able to monitor the two young people.

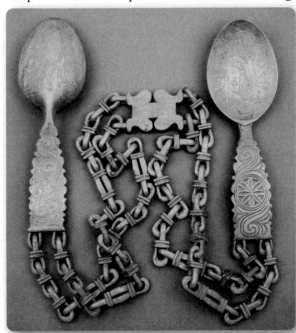

The linked wedding spoons carved from one block of wood, signed and dated, from Hjartdal, Telemark, 1923.

Tradition was that the suitor had to carve the spoons intended for the young woman out of one block of wood. The spoons were connected together with a hand-carved wooden chain. The spoons were then hung over the door of their new home. Yet another tradition of rejection was the admonition to watch out for "the wife who wears spoons around her neck when her husband is away from home." Spoons hanging around her neck indicated the wife was not happy with her relationship with her husband and was seeking other relationships.

Engagement Rings and the Betrothal

According to Rev. Fredrick Metcalfe who wrote in his journal in 1856:

> "The betrothal (a pledge to marry) was a very important affair in Norway. When the woman became engaged, the custom for a young woman was to exchange rings with her fiancé. The rings were retained permanently and no additional ring was placed on the finger of the bride at the marriage ceremony." [In contrast to the custom in the U.S.][14]

A typical farm wedding in Voss, Norway in 1858, with the bridal couple at the altar. Note the bridal crown of the Voss region and the *prestekrage* (pastor's ruffed). Lithograph from an 1859 painting by K. Bergslien.

An important participant in Norwegian marriage was the Lutheran pastor. In the Norwegian Lutheran State Church marriage included two distinct ceremonies: the betrothal, followed later by the wedding ceremony. The betrothal could precede the other generally for one, two or three years. The betrothal ceremony vows were recited and the couple joined hands with the pastor. The future father-in-law of the bride to-be and the witnesses placed their hands on the couple's.

Even after Norway was converted to Lutheranism in 1537, the ceremony remained very much intact, except the pastor was asked to recite the betrothal ceremony vows. Eventually the words were changed to resemble those spoken at the marriage ceremony. The completion of the betrothal ceremony was celebrated with a large dinner at the bride's home.

The bride is seated sidesaddle on a white horse, with family and friends gathered around, excited to join the procession to the church. The painting depicts the village of Eidsfjord, Sogn og Fjordane, by Nils Bergslein, 1892.

Choosing a Time and Date for the Wedding

Most weddings were held in the spring or in June or July. Weddings in the summer could be larger because travel was easier and guests could easily return to their homes if the weather were favorable. In autumn or winter, the daylight hours were short and only a limited number of guests could sleep in the host's house. Another factor could be cold weather, making it inconvenient to stay in outbuildings; therefore many guests would have to go home in the dark and return each day. Finally there was the reality that the food supply was limited in the unproductive off-seasons.

The wedding ceremony was held on a weekday except for Mondays and Thursdays. The superstitious notion was that if the wedding were held on the first day of the week, it would soon have to be held again because one of the couple would die and the other would have to remarry. (Norwegian calendars are different from

American so that Monday, not Sunday, is the first day of the week.) Also, in some areas of the country, marriage on *torstag* (Thursday) was believed to be unfavorable because of the superstition that the date would lead to conflict in the couple's married life. In other districts, Saturday weddings were discouraged because they would disturb the peace of the weekend and would cause people to miss church services. In many areas then, only Tuesday, Wednesday or Friday were appropriate days on which to have a wedding ceremony.[15]

Setesdalsinteriør (The interior of a home in Setesdal) has open-hearth fireplace letting smoke escape through a hole in the ceiling, thus making the ceiling black with soot. 1860 painting by Olaf Isaachsen, Photo by J. Lathion.

Early Planning

Weddings have always taken on great social importance, particularly in rural folk art areas of the country such as Valdres, Sogn og Fordane, Telemark and Gudbrands-dalen. Planning for the wedding began when the daughter was quite young, usually at confirmation, around 14 years of age. In anticipation of a wedding, a trunk became a prized family heirloom passed down to future generations. The young girl, with her mother's guidance, would start building her *trousseau* by making needle work, embroidery and Hardanger stitching to enhance napkins, scarves, pillow cases, blankets and other items for setting up a home. She would work on the project over the years, always increasing the complexity to show off her skill.

A daughter might receive a family trunk or the father could make a new one especially for this event. A trunk provided a place to keep handmade items. Many times it was painted with decorative *rosemaling* along with the name or initials of the daughter and her birth date.

Invitation to the Wedding

The invitation to the wedding was given at least 14 days before the ceremony and it followed a traditional set speech. An older man in the community, perhaps a teacher or postmaster, or the groom himself dressed in his best clothes, was the *bear-mann* (the official inviter). He would ride to the farms of those invited and give a formal invitation speech, seated on his horse. Here is a formal speech from Hallingdal:

> *I am bringing a friendly greeting, prayer and invitation to you from Martin Hjulmaker Olson Berg and Marit Oldsdatter Ellendshaugen that you will give them the pleasure to come as their guests, both young and old, all who can be free. You can take your horses and there will be no cost [meaning the host will provide the shelter and water, but guests had to bring along their own feed].*

Hardangerfele (Hardanger fiddle) belonging to Jon Ellefson Steinkjondalen is signed and dated 1871. Note the carved lion's head, mother of pearl bone inlay and pen scroll design—all-important characteristics of the fiddle.

Without charging for minor expenses, there were two ways to cover the costs of the wedding: contributed food (*sendingsbryllup*) was brought by the guests and was used for meals at the wedding and second, gifts of money (*Skålelag*), whereby guests give both food and money to the bride and groom.

Hardanger Fiddle in the Norwegian Folk Wedding

A Norwegian folk wedding would be incomplete without including the *Hardangerfele* (Hardanger fiddle) at the top of the list. This uniquely Norwegian instrument is very different from the classical violin. Four of the eight strings are played with a bow and four to five below pick up the sound and vibrate in resonance, in a sound similar to a bagpipe. Around 1550 in the Hardanger Valley, the Hardanger fiddle was invented and the model spread throughout Norway, becoming a national instrument.

> The Hardanger fiddle also has structural differences from the classical violin including a shorter neck and a higher arching of the top. It is decorated with mother-of-pearl and bone inlay and with rosing (a black floral design). The materials are spruce, maple, and ebony. Sometimes an animal head, such as a lion, is used at the very end of the fiddle instead of a scroll. The length is 25 inches and the width is seven inches, on average.

Services held in a Norwegian farmers' church with the *klokker* leading the singing of hymns. The pastor to the extreme left was lighting the candles. Painting by Adolph Tidemand in 1845.

Wedding music was played before and during the wedding procession as well as at dances after the ceremony. Fiddle tunes for dancing could also be sung, called *slåtter*. Many of these tunes, adopted in the U.S., were taken from folk melodies sung in rural Norway. In Norway, the dance music is in 2/4 time and called the *gangar;* the *springar* type is referred to as 3/4 time. Fiddlers usually mark the rhythm by tapping the beat with their feet.[16]

🎻In Norwegian folklore, fiddle music was often associated with the devil or some other supernatural being. According to folk tales, good fiddlers were taught by the devil himself and all fiddlers were seen as troublemakers. The church denounced the instrument as one of the devil because it was played at dances and drinking parties. Otto Rindlisbacher of Rice Lake, Wisconsin made fun of this tradition by painting three red "dancing devils" with horns, forked tails and long spears on the side of his Hardanger fiddle.[16]

Dans i Setesdal (Dance in Setesdal), 1891 painting by Gustav Wentzel features both dancers in typical Setesdal *bunader* and fiddler playing music fit for a hot summer day.

🎻With a normal fiddle, you use catgut to make the strings of the violin but for the strings of the Hardanger fiddle, you use the whole cat.

—Fiddlers' adage

Guests Always Included in a Wedding

Certain people were always present at weddings. Obviously, the bride and groom had *brudepike og brudesvenn* (a maid of honor and a groomsman), respectively. (The tradition today in Norway is that children are chosen to be *brudepike* and *brudesvenn*.) The *forlover* (the one standing up for the bride and groom) is legally required for both bride and groom, while b*rudepike* and *brudesvenn* are optional.

The *brudekone* (bride's helper) was an older woman who was in charge of helping to dress the bride. The *kjellermann* (tapster) was responsible for tapping the keg and passing around ale and spirits. *Mor i buret* (a good cook in the community) was the cook in charge, a term used in 1800s, for the head cook in all festive gatherings. The role of *spillemann* (fiddler) was important and could vary by region.

For example, he might be asked to play at the bride's home, the march to the church and for dances and receptions, but not in the church.

The most unique role was the *kjøkemester* (master of ceremonies). The role came from an earlier period when a *hovmester (maître d'hôtel)* was responsible for the king's food and drink. He was a person who could have served as master of ceremonies for weddings, baptisms confirmations and funerals. He kept things organized and saw that all the people were informed about the agenda using prepared remarks based on cue cards.

Kjøkemester welcomes guests at the door of the church, with fiddler and clarinetist at the right and a little boy with noise maker at far left.

An early record of a *kjøkemester* leading a town wedding in was in 1552 in Bergen, indicating the ancient nature of these wedding traditions. The first recorded farm wedding was in 1620, also in Bergen. Even today the custom of having a *kjøkemester* is followed in some parts of the country.

A folk wedding is a series of planned activities culminating in a ceremony in which the clothing, gifts, food and traditions were conceived of and handmade by rural, landless, Norwegian peasant farmers.

CHAPTER 4

FOLK WEDDING CEREMONIES:
THE INFLUENCE OF FAMILY, RELATIVES AND FRIENDS

The wedding ceremony was the culmination of the process that unfolded over a long period of time, from the first wedding item made by the bride when she was young. This chapter deals with the most significant activities related to this event.

Nattefrieri (night visiting) was a way for boys to visit girls in the girl's bedroom to get better acquainted. Drawing by Joachim Frich.

Major Elements in Norwegian Folk Wedding Ceremonies

Throughout Norway, people in rural areas had their own local or regional wedding customs. In large part, these traditions were unwritten guidelines or instructions, including those told to them by church pastors, friends or their families. Anyone intending to marry was expected to follow wedding customs carefully. A photographic exhibition in the *Hardanger og Voss Folkemuseum* in Voss (a small village in Hordaland county between Hardanger and Sogn og Fjordane), explains 35 steps that were taken in preparation for Norwegian folk weddings in Voss in the 1800s.[1] Some of these elements include: how to select one's mate, the courtship, the engagement, pre- and post- wedding celebrations, dowry, music, wedding dress, jewelry, food, wedding procession and the marriage ceremony. The following sections describe some of the topics used in the Voss photographic exhibit.[17]

> 🐝 No man's costume was complete without a knife with carvings, silver work and a handsome sheath. In addition to knives, a man's costume was embellished with silver buttons and silk kerchiefs.

Dans i Setesdal (Dance in Setesdal), 1891 painting by Gustav Wentzel features both dancers in typical Setesdal *bunader* and fiddler playing music fit for a hot summer day.

Evening Before Wedding

The evening before the wedding, the groom led a procession of men to the bride's home. Their purpose was to take her to the groom's residence, where she would spend the night and dress for the wedding ceremony the next day. At the same time, family from out of the area would arrive to be housed with parents of the bride or groom. Other guests arrived the next morning bringing along their contribution to the party's food supply *(føring)*. The food was carried in wooden or woven containers appropriate for the type of food. These containers would have been fashioned by local rosemaling artists, woodcarvers and basket makers.

Superstitions and the Weather

In all farming communities, the weather was on everybody's mind before the wedding. By superstition, rain or snow on the bride's hair meant good luck, so people wished for some rain either on the way to church or on the way back. Many other superstitions were commonly found. In some districts, to avoid bad luck, the wedding procession took a different route to and from the church. If this were not possible, the procession would make a loop around the farmyard called the *brudes-vingen* (to travel around the home of the bride and groom) so the path would not be the same. It was thought necessary to do this circular route so the evil forces would be fooled and not follow the bridal party. When the party entered the farmyard, the bride would drink from a wooden bowl. She then would throw the bowl over the roof of the farmhouse. If the bowl landed right side up, the bride would die before the groom. If it landed upside down, the groom would die first.

Fire Hardangerfeler (Four Hardanger fiddle players) lead the bridal procession to the church with the bride and groom on horseback followed by a long line of relatives and friends all in *bunader.*

The Host's Home

Cleaning and decorating the various houses and rooms were important activities. Floors were swept, scoured and strewn with juniper twigs for a fresh scent and festive look. Tapestries and other wall hangings were brought out of the family trunk and hung on exterior walls. Specially made cushions were placed on seats of chairs and benches for guests. Dinnerware was borrowed from friends and neighbors along with extra tables and benches. Arrangements were made with neighbors to host overnight guests.

Of great importance was the bridal bedchamber, hung with tapestries and skin blankets. The bed and bedding were made with the finest sheets and *dyne* (feather quilt) the parents could find. The hosts would carefully go over the entire property looking for flaws that wedding guests could use to criticize the management of the household.

Gathering of Horses and Noise Makers to Process to the Church

In the summer time, weddings were planned for 4:00 p.m. at the church and in the fall or winter at 3:00 p.m. From 11:00 a.m. to noon the fiddler's *slåttet* (dance melodies), with accompaniment of a drummer, would begin in front of the host's house, usually the bride's parent's home. This was the time when the guests arrived. The *kjøkemester* would receive them at the door, and they would proceed inside to greet the hosts and the bridal couple. The *kjellermann* would serve ale and alcohol, and when all the guests had arrived, a meal would follow.

For the main wedding meal, the couple sat at the head of the table with their parents on each side. Guests were to be seated according to their social rank within the community and family. The *kjøkemester* kept track of the local hierarchy and would then tell the people where to sit so that nobody would be offended. He was also the person who would lead the table prayer and would sing or lead everyone in song after the meal.

After the meal, the procession to the church would form outside the house. The bride was helped on the horse and the groom would walk along side, leading the horse. The *kjøkemester* was always first in line, followed by the *spillemann* (fiddler). The positions of the bride and groom in the procession varied by district. In some areas, they sat with each other, and in others, they were separated on the way to church and then brought together after the ceremony on the return to the farm. In many cases, horses were used, and the procession was organized with light colored horses ahead of the dark ones. White horses would stand out in a crowd more and white was a symbol of the purity of the bride. The bride would always ride the white horse, if one were available.

The whole procession was surrounded with noise and disturbances. One group, usually young men, would beat drums or fire pistols or rifles in the air, riding back and forth from the farm to the church before the procession started out. Noisemakers and the advance party had a traditional purpose in mind, namely, to protect the bride from evil spirits who were believed to be dangerous, especially on her wedding day.

Haugianerne (a Haugean meeting depicting lay preacher Hans Nielson Hauge, an exponent of the simple life). Painting is by A. Tidemand in 1848 and is in the *Kunstmuseet*, Düsseldorf, Germany.

Church Ceremony

Guests entered the church in the order in which they arrived. The groom and male guests sat on the right side of the church and the bride and the women and children on the left (as viewed from the entry looking toward the altar). The bride and the groom met at the altar, where the service and vows followed the Lutheran worship texts commonly used at this period of time.

The wedding rites were recited; the couple joined hands. At the time of the exchange of vows, the parents placed their hands on those of the bride and groom as witnesses. These vows included admonitions to love, honor and obey, prayers for children and for an overall fruitful life together. Again, superstition was in evidence, even regarding the church services and celebration. In some places, it was said that the one who knelt first at the altar railing would be the first to die. Another tradition was that the first one to look at his/her spouse on the second day of the wedding festivities would get the upper hand in their relationship. Immediately after the service,

A rosemaled hymnbook box in the 1800s was sometimes carried by the bride during the wedding ceremony. The groom would carry a small book, most likely passages from Scripture.

In this photo, the box is lying on a crocheted table cloth which is a type of needle work in which loops of a thread are interwoven by means of a single hooked needle. The tablecloth is large enough to cover a table with twelve seated guests and was made by Marie Bjerkness over a two-year period of time, crocheting the same round pattern over and over again to make the hundreds of round designs.

the wedding party gave a monetary offering to the pastor and the *klokker* (sexton who may have led singing and may have been the local school master). To give an offering, the bride and the groom would lead the bridal party to pass in back of the altar, a long tradition still honored today in some Lutheran churches in the U.S. and was true especially to collect money for special events. Money for the pastor would be laid on the altar and the money for the *klokker* would be laid on his chair. They, in turn, would nod their heads and express their thanks.

At that point the whole wedding party, in procession, would continue on to the farm of the bride, the bride and the groom riding beside each other as husband

Interiør fra en bondestue (Interior of a room in a farm home), A. Tidemand painting in oil in 1848.

and wife. The word for the earlier celebration before the wedding itself was the *festarøl*. Judging by the word, *øl*, meaning beer or ale, drinking was an important part of the celebration.[18]

🐦 Festerøl was celebrated at the time the couple was engaged, not at the time of marriage. An engagement was a legally binding official act.

The Banquet

The *mor i buret* (the woman who prepared the dinner) met the newly wedded couple and bridal party at the door. The *kjøkemester* invited everyone to the table. Welcoming speeches, songs, jokes and toasts were made to the bride and groom. Some speeches would have moral overtones; others would be humorous or practical.

Choices at the dinner would depend upon the time of year and the area of the country. In general, the main course was *rømmegrøt* (sour cream porridge), along with other dishes followed by a dessert, *riskrem* (rice porridge). Much of the meal was made from dairy products such as cream, milk and cheese. Thin *flatbrød* (flatbread) was usually baked on a griddle and made from wheat or oats. Crisp bread made from rye, was prepared in advance in large quantities and could be stored indefinitely. Rolls or bread made fresh that day might be included.

Fresh meat, fish or game was served when available, but the main course would usually be dried or smoked meats, preserved in the fall and intended to last for the whole year. *Rømmegrøt* would be served together with *spekemat* (dried, cured meat) and flatbread. *Fårekøtt* (mutton), *skinke* (cured or smoked ham) or salami-like sausages were other options.

On the seacoast, fresh fish, smoked, cured, and dried fish might prevail over the choice of meat. Weddings in the late summer or fall could include fresh or boiled vegetables such as parsnips, turnips, rutabagas, cabbage and carrots. Beer or ale was served as well as hard liquor.

Bryllupsdrakten (wedding outfit) from Hardanger with groom holding a Viking spear to fend off evil spirits. Lithograph by Johan Fr. Eckersberg, 1852 print by C. Tonsberg.

Kransekake (wreath cake)

Sweets or various cakes played a prominent role in the wedding feasts. Among the cakes, *kransekake* (wreath cake) was prominent. This cake is a very traditional Norwegian dessert eaten at weddings to complement the bride's wedding crown. The cake has been called many other names: *tårnkake* (tower cake or ring or Viking wedding cake). Also, an original variant used at weddings was *overflødighetshorn* (horn of abundance or cornucopia, filled with chocolate cookies and other small treats).

Kransekake to this day is made with almonds, sugar and egg whites and decorated with icing and small Norwegian flags. Sometimes a bottle of wine or *akevitt* (potato liqueur) is placed in the center.

Donations to the Bride and Groom

The wedding celebration was a major event that could last many days, with eating, visiting, playing games and dancing, as has already been mentioned. At a specific day and time called *skålelag* (giving of gifts and money), the *kjøkemester,* when he thought the time was right, would take a large wooden bowl, pound it on the table and invite each guest to put gifts of money into the bowl. The *kjøkemester* loudly announced the name of each guest, revealing the amount of money each guest gave, and expressed his thanks on behalf of the bride and groom.

This custom of open fundraising was criticized in historical writings because it was also used for other church holidays to raise money. People knew that they would be singled out and should give generously. As a consequence, the poor were always embarrassed. Also, sometimes the host would put out as little food as possible and then offer the guests as much to drink as possible just before the time of the collection of gifts. After the 1850s, the *skålelag* went out of style. A later alternative approach developed which was to send food for the dinner to the couple.

Meaning of *Bryllup* (wedding dance)

According to custom at the wedding dance, the first dance was for the bride and groom. Another tradition was to have the bride and groom participate in a simple line dance. Early in the 1800s, the bride was the one who led the young women's line dance called *Bryllup* or "dancing out of the maidens." The dance involved holding hands and forming a long line. The group then danced through rooms in the house, across the farmyard and around farm buildings.

The dancers might sing or have fiddlers play, but neither was necessary. The bride was "danced out" meaning she no longer belonged with the young people. Some folklorists believe the word *bryllup* (bride's run or dance or line dance) comes from dancing the "long dance" for the last time and then being excluded from the young people. Others think the word refers to the "run" when people arrived (ran) to watch the bride being taken to her new home.

Wedding-day at Troldhaugen

by E. Grieg (1843–1907)

After the "long dance," young and old joined the dance. At first the party would keep to a courtly style, but as the evening wore on and the older folks retired or gathered in another room to visit, the younger people took over the dancing floor. The party became increasingly wild as dancers and fiddlers became energized by the excitement of the festivities and the alcohol.

En søndag eftermiddag i en Hardangersk røkstue (A Sunday afternoon in a Hardanger smokehouse). Painting by Adolph Tidemand and photo by O. Væring.

At one point in the evening guests would assemble to follow the newlyweds by torchlight to the bridal loft. Sometimes the bride would hide and a frenzied search to find her would begin. After the bride was discovered, the procession would proceed to the bridal bedchamber. The procession then returned to the party and the revelers soon returned to dancing, with everybody becoming more and more energized. The festivities died down at some time in the morning when the guests became exhausted. The younger group, however, would often stay up all night; they wanted as much fun as possible because the dance was a welcome relief, taking them away from their long, hard workdays.

For a traditional folk wedding described in the early 1800s, the bride's slip or underclothes and the groom's shirt were to be new and never worn before the wedding and only one time afterwards: at their deaths the man and women would wear these garments as grave clothes for their burial.

Pa kyrkjebakken (In the churchyard) was painted by Nils Bergslien (1853-1928) who was born in Voss. All the married women in this painting wear the Hardanger *bunader*. Bergslien is known for depicting ordinary, everyday life of different types of people. Photo by O. Væring.

The Honeymoon

The honeymoon in Norway at this time was called *hvetebrødsdager* (white bread days), indicating the popularity of bleached bread as a delicacy. Dark bread is ordinary, eaten in daily life. Rarely did the newlyweds want to leave town, but spent this period of time with their family and friends and putting their new home in order.

The whole family turns out to help move the bride's trunk and boxes to her new home. Painting by Andreas Askevold, 1860. Photo by J. Lathion.

Norwegian folk art is by definition, handmade art crafted by the "common people" in Norway, the family of a tenant farmer, living in a remote, rural area of Norway. The majority of people in Norway in the 1800s were landless sharecroppers. These farmers created folk art as an expression of their interests in making utilitarian and beautiful objects for the household.

CHAPTER 5

FOLK ARTIFACTS, RURAL FARMER-SHARECROPPERS CREATE PIECES OF FOLK ART

The tenant farmers' creation of folk art was expressed through very practical household items like carved decorations on furniture, rosemaled ceilings and walls, carved or painted boxes for carrying personal items, tapestries for gifts at christenings and weddings or artistic iron works for doors, mainly to hold keys and latches. These folk expressions were formed over a long time period, beginning with pagan and Christian art.

The bride is wearing a gold *brudekrona* and carrying a *handaklede* (handmade, embroidered, hand covering). The couple is from Hjørundfjord på Sunnmøre coming home from church. Lithograph by Johan Fr. Eckersberg, printed by Chr. Tonsberg, 1852.

Influence of Christian Art

Pagan art of the Viking period was gradually transformed by the Christian church after the year 1000. At first Norwegian craftsmen, especially wood carvers, were personally aloof to the Christian churches, but as they gained confidence in the priests and the institution, they adopted more and more new religious art forms. One of the first Christian motifs adopted was the grapevine, an important Christian symbol, (from the *Bible,* John 15:5, "I am the vine, you are the branches)." These symbols were easily adapted to fit on posts, columns and doorways.

Yet another plant motif was the elegant Mediterranean

acanthus flower, found in Italy as a design on the top of Roman Corinthian columns. The flower was a thistle-like plant with long, white or colored spikes, enhancing the acanthus leaf. The acanthus flower soon became the central figure in the northern style of art and appears all though the various forms of art, be it carving or painting.

Later in the medieval period, wood carvers accepted a rather simplified version of the Gothic rosette motif, the diminutive form of a rose. In art, it is a painted or sculpted ornament, usually in circles, having petals that leave the center, radiating symmetrically outward. However, it was not until the 18th century that rosemalers appeared to revive memories of past Gothic and Viking symbols. They also added the well-liked animal motifs of the horse, lion or dragon and mixed many of these themes together.

Throughout Europe, the Crusades from the 11th to the 13th century popularized other symbols: the large, powerful lion and the eagle with sharp vision and powerful wings. Another symbol of power was the Oriental dragon. The dragon was seen as a mythical monster usually represented as a large reptile with wings and claws, breathing fire and smoke. The head of the dragon is found especially on the prow of Viking ships and on the gables of stave churches. All these symbols were represented in church art and generally were placed on plaques on walls and around windows and doorways. Usually the lion is shown in battle but it appeared more domesticated as time passed. The dragon, in later times, finally was shown as a crescent (quarter moon) with the lion standing on top of him, triumphant.[19]

The interlaced ribbon motif became as important as other figures, almost a national symbol of Norway. These plaited motifs (braided or interwoven) provided a firm basis taken from the French-inspired ribbon work of the Rococo period. Monograms, figures made up of two or more letters combined in simple designs, were very popular on silver brooches in the eighteenth and nineteenth centuries. All these Romanesque patterns such as the vine, the animals and the intertwined ribbons, became so firmly established in Norwegian folk art that Gothic styles never had as significant an impact in Norway as they might have.

> 🐝 Folk artist versus folk craftsman: A person skilled in the mechanics of his art but lacking artistry is a craftsman. In contrast, a folk artist is a person skilled in both mechanics of the work and its artistic rendering. To judge the difference is sometimes a very difficult task.

The plainly geometric character of the Gothic rosette was somewhat evident in *karveskurd* (chip carving). Chip carving consists of square, triangular, circular or star-shaped geometric patterns sketched out with a ruler and compass. The designs are chipped out of the flat surface of wood or stone using a small knife or chisel. Chip carving was used to some extent on furniture and was also generally employed in decorating doorways, small wooden boxes, *mangletre,* trunks, burial caskets, knife handles and on church altar pieces and baptismal fonts. Chip carving designs were also combined with the Romanesque vine. The fan-shaped sections looked like the palmetto motif (palm tree branch) and may have been influenced by it. A reason for certain recurring motifs was the fact that some buildings and stave churches from the Middle Ages were still standing, serving as accessible models for any particular style.

Two factors kept several medieval traditions alive in Norway and isolated from the world. The first was the inaccessibility of many farms in isolated river valleys. The second was that communication with the outside world remained generally very primitive, mostly by footpaths over the mountains that were difficult to cross even in good weather. In the interior, a network of walking, riding and cart paths wound through the forest and rocky slopes of many valley bottoms, connecting small villages not seen often by many outsiders.

The couple is wearing *bunader* from Øst-Telemark, with the hem of woman's black skirt overlaid with some very dominant red and green colors.

Folk Costume Tradition: the *Bunad,* from the Old Ways to the New

Some may think that the *bunad* (translated broadly as gear, clothes, outfits or costumes) is a women's dress, but in fact, it is a distinctive type of clothing worn by men, women and children in Norway's fishing and farming communities. A distinction should be made between a *bunad* and a folk costume. The folk costume was clothing worn for everyday life and work around the farm. Parts of the folk costume could be the same as a *bunad,* but had little decoration, and were often shop-worn.

Hardanger costumes from left to right: an old man dressed in clothes resembling those worn in the Middle Ages, holding a falcon and an ax for protection from evil spirits; a young woman with typical hair arrangement for an unmarried pike; the bride with crown, decorated bodice, red skirt, apron and embroidered hand covering; the bridegroom in his best clothes, with decorated hair, hat, and cravat tucked into his shirt; a child, dressed like an adult; a woman dressed as a newly-married wife on the first Sunday in church after the marriage ceremony with a white shirt, white apron and jacket and married woman's headdress. Johannes Flintoe. Watercolor. 1822.

🐝 Generally folk dress communicated in various ways the sex, age, status, and occupation of the wearer and place of origin. Worn on special occasions, it emphasized the solemnity of the event.

Certain parts of the *bunad* worn in one area could have arisen from models of different areas of the country and/or other historical periods. Medieval and European clothing and Renaissance fashions had some influence, but the design, the use of color and the way of combining these elements were predominantly local. At the end of the 19th century the daily use of the folk costume was reduced and eventually almost discontinued by nearly the whole population.[21]

The modern *bunad* movement had its beginnings in the 19th century with the advent of national romanticism. Neighboring countries such as Denmark and Sweden, and more notably, Germany, were also interested in folk clothing. The *dirndls* for women and *lederhosen* for men of Bavaria in southern Germany remain popular to current times and were very visible during the 1972 Munich Olympics. *Bunad* traditions also are connected to folk costumes, such that if a woman wears her apron strings tied on the left, it signals that she is single while apron strings tied on the right, declare that she is in a relationship. In Norway the *bunad* had a

Spenne (buckle) on the shoe sometimes has a square design for men and is oval-shaped for women. Their socks highlight the design on the buckle.

Women's vests or bodices are embroidered and, in most cases, on both the front and back. Stord, Hordaland is a county that boasts of the largest variety of *bunader*. At a 1998 Bergen Festival, 120 different *bunader* were displayed just from the Hordaland and Sogn og Fjordane areas.

more lasting impact because of pre-industrial Norway's relative isolation from other areas of its own country and from its nearby neighbors of Sweden and Denmark.

🐾 It is estimated that two and a half million Norwegians own *bunader* but they are only worn on average 2.25 times a year. Fifty-five percent of Norwegian women own a *bunad* but only seven percent of Norwegian men own one. Despite individual variations, a more unified style for a particular area most likely is a result of attending the same church.[21]

Folk costumes and sometimes *bunader* were made from coarse, loosely woven homespun, an integral part of rural making of clothes. Homespun was not used in large cities. As has been mentioned before, in the early 1800s, Norway was a truly rural society, with only two cities over 20,000, Bergen and Kristiania (Oslo). The *husmann* clothes, worn every day, had little decoration, but clothing used for attending special occasions, such as church services or weddings, had varying amounts of decoration, but mainly embroidery. Embroidery might be considered the female artistic version of rosemaling, which represents the male tradition at this period of time.

🐾 The present Queen of Norway, Sonja Haraldsen, her daughter, Märtha Louise, and daughter-in-law, Mette-Marit, all wear *bunads* at special events such as *syttende mai*. Queen Sonja and her daughter, Märtha Louise, wear East Telemark *bunader*. Telemark is the ancestral home of the Queen. Because Mårtha Louise owns reindeer, she is also allowed to wear the Saami equivalent of the *bunad:* the *gakti.*

In front of the Domkirke in Oslo, Princess Mette-Marit, Prince Haakon Magnus, their children Prince Sverre Magnus and Princess Ingrid Alexandra (second in line to be the reigning monarch of Norway after her father Haakon), as well as Mette-Marit's son, Marius Borg Høiby, are well attired in *bunader*, while the family dog, Milly Kakao, sports a festive ribbon around her neck.

A German traveler once wrote, "There hides an artist in each Norwegian farmer." This was especially true of the farmer's wife, who would spend countless hours adding colored yarns, beads and tatting. There were other variations added to white work that she had woven with her own hands. She did this work with a sensitive feeling for colors and patterns. When her own sense was less sure, she could refer to the work of her mother, grandmother or other relatives. Over time, designs were improved, the less pleasing elements were eliminated and good designs retained.

🐝 Norwegian tatting was fine lace made by looping and knotting thread on a hand shuttle. This device carries the lower thread back and forth in making a strong lock stitch. Tatting is generally used for edging or hemming.

A woman's *bunad* was the most striking element of a Norwegian folk wedding. An individual's home district, age, social status and occupation could be identified by its style and color. *Bunader* made in Valdres, Gudsbrandsdalen and Hallingdal, all counties in the interior of a mountainous countryside, as well as Telemark, stood apart because of people's lack of contact with other districts of the country.

Sometimes referred to as the national *bunad* of Norway, the Hardanger outfit, was made in a uniform, standardized way: a red vest, black skirt with a white apron embellished by embroidery or ribbons or both. A short jacket of black brocade (a rich cloth with a raised designs of silk, velvet, gold or silver) woven into it and covered with a frontispiece of scarlet cloth. The dress was usually elaborately decorated.

🐝 British Princess Maud, in 1896, married Danish Prince Carl (later, King Haakon VII) in the chapel of Buckingham Palace, England. When she became Queen of Norway in 1905, she thought the Hardanger *bunad* so beautiful that she had one made for herself. She wore it many times at events in Norway during her reign from 1905 to 1938.

Queen Maud in the 1900s was fascinated by the Hardanger costume and wore it on special occasions. During this period of time, the Hardanger costume was the Norwegian "national" costume.

Princess Märtha Louise is an accomplished folk dancer. She is wearing a Setesdal costume at a dance competition in Oslo in August 1992. Leikaringer (groups of folk dancers) are located all over Norway. *Kappleiken* are folk musician contests, with musicians who play traditional instruments such as the Norwegian zither, the Jew's harp and the Hardanger fiddle.

Most frequently, the bodice, the top of the dress, was adorned with many necklaces or the national ornament called a *sølje,* a circular, silver- gilded brooch. (To silver-guild a brooch is to overlay it with a thin layer of silver or gold. This addition makes it appear bright and attractive and perhaps of greater value.) The brooch is an ornamental pin with a clasp, typically measuring three inches in diameter, with 20 gilded silver droplets attached to the edges most likely to serve as a symbol of embroidery. To compliment the brooch, an elaborate leather belt also with silver droplets is added to woman's waist.

In some rural areas, people have preserved the styles, colors and construction of the *bunad* used during the 1800s. Others, however, changed their patterns and accessories, influenced in part by European fashions, while others simply wanted to make changes to their *bunader* to be free from restraints of the past. Design changes have been made as late as 1970 and, most likely, will continue.

🐝 The traditional headgear for married women was made out of fine linen. Being "scarfed as a wife" was an important rite of passage. A married woman's hair had to be completely covered in the headgear. Long flowing hair was an important addition to a wedding dress and a way of adding an exotic aspect to the bride.

A Valdres-style *bunad* has a highly decorated hem on the skirt and on the front of the vest. The colors and designs are highlighted on a dark blue or black fabric. As far as possible, *bunader* are made of natural material: linen or cotton for shirts; silk for cravats, vests and bodices and wool for jackets, trousers and stockings. A *bunad* is unfinished when appropriate shoes and stockings do not match the rest of the outfit. One of the early *bunad* advocates said, "You can't be traditional in the middle and modern at both ends."

On the other hand, today, people are discouraged from modifying the traditional *bunad*. A concerted effort has been made to go back to the styles of the 1800s. In the middle of the 20th century, there was a demand to establish a standardized, district-wide *bunad* board to help make these decisions. As a result, Norwegians, for the most part, now have access to an official institution, the *Landsnemda for Bunadspørsmål* (a national committee to put *bunad* making on the right track), founded in 1947. Norwegians can now also seek advice from the *Bunad* and Folk Costume Advisory Board located in Valdres, Norway. Due to the heated discussions about the status of the *bunad*, it is difficult to state the number of different types of *bunader* in Norway, but some estimate that around 400 distinctive styles remain today according to *Norsk Bunadleksikon* 2006.

Many districts in Norway have set up *bunad*-making courses to ensure that *bunader* are made correctly according to the historic designs, colors and trim materials. Norwegians are now taking immense pride in their folk heritage and have personal satisfaction in wearing a traditional *bunad*.

Brud og brudepike fra Vossevangen (Bride and Bridesmaid from Vossevangen) by A.Tidemand, 1855.

Bunader are expensive to buy or make now, as in the past. Hundreds of hours of work are put into the complicated embroideries on skirts, aprons, bodices, shirts and hats. Many people attempt to make their own outfits to save money, purchasing patterns and material from *Husfliden* or *Heimen* stores. Professional dressmakers, as well, sell their outfits on their own or through these businesses located throughout Norway. A complete *bunad* can cost thousands of dollars (estimates are from $6,000 to $10,000), including buying jewelry, belts, buckle shoes and other accessories.

One good reason for owning a *bunad,* however, is that it will always remain in style for *syttende mai* (Norwegian Constitution Day) or other events such as baptisms, confirmations, weddings, funerals and private parties. Norwegian-Americans who buy traditional *bunader* have found the heavy wool fabric insufferably hot. A cotton summer *bunad* is an alternative found in attractive sky-blue and rose-embroidered styles from the Telemark region, or the colorful checkered *bunad* found in the extended valley of Hallingdal.

🌺 Turid Liss Agersborg of *Husfliden* in Oslo is a contemporary Norwegian *bunad* maker. She said that today there are more home-produced *bunader* for men than for women.

Sella Larsdatter (Sella, Lars' Daughter) by A. Tidemand in 1871. She is dressed in a child's Hardanger *bunad* and is overwhelmed with the distinction.

The bridegroom's clothing was far less elaborate than the bride's. He would wear either knee breeches or long trousers, as well as a vest and dress jacket with buttons of silver or pewter. He would round out his outfit with some kind of hat, gloves or mittens made for the occasion by the bride. He wore a long-sleeved white shirt, foulard and shoes with buckles.

Hulda Garborg (1862-1934) and Klara Semb (1884-1970) were driving forces behind the movement to encourage the use of folk costumes, based on traditions from various regions of Norway. Garborg's interest arose from a dance group she formed in Oslo, as she wanted to create dance costumes for the ensemble. In early productions, the dancers wore a simplified Hardanger *bunad*. As described before, their outfit consisted of a red vest with beaded breastplate, black skirt, white apron with Hardanger lace and a long-sleeved, white shirt.

This costume was often printed on postcards, depicting young women in unlikely situations such as milking cows or raking hay in the mountains. Hulda Garborg, herself, wore a colorful costume from Gol in Hallingdal. She helped simplify the costumes so they would be more easily used for dancing. The dance group performed for the first time in 1900, touring both in Norway and abroad. Eventually, she wrote her first book about *bunader* in 1903: *Norsk Klædebunad (Notes on Norwegian Bunader)*. She pioneered the modern preservation of Norway's cultural heritage and her work inspired others to create authentic regional *Bunader*, both in Norway and among Norwegian-Americans in the U.S.

🦢 Folk dress provided evidence of a group sense of identity. It is a major bearer of tradition and adheres to certain un-written rules regarding use of color and pattern of weaving, embroidery, knitting and of design in accessories such as brooches, buttons and buckles. Buckle shoes were common as early as the 1300s.

🦢 Rigid heddles (A series of parallel strips of wood carved out of a thin piece of wood equipped with eyelets and used for separating and guiding the warp threads) were often used for weaving hair bands or belts.

The Bridal Crown, *Brudekrone*

The *brudekrone* (bridal crown) traditionally one of the most expensive accessories of the wedding *Bunader*, came into use in Norway at the end of the Middle Ages. Drawing on church practices, the *krone* was inspired by portrayals of crowns worn by

Jesus and the Virgin Mary. The medieval church was still Roman Catholic and thus the near-worship of the Virgin Mary played an important part in church dogma and practice, with great impact on women in the church.

This Virgin Mary emphasis changed greatly with the advent of the Reformation in 1537, but the tradition of wearing a marriage crown lived on. It was the crown worn by the Virgin Mary, especially, that was the inspiration for young women to wear a holy crown at their marriage ceremonies. For the family, the crown became a symbol of purity and virginity. Women who did not merit this distinction or were pregnant were permitted only to wear a small crown or a type of *hodeplagg* (head

Hardangerbrud (Hardanger bride) by A. Tidemand, 1849. The bodice is decorated with beads, lace and metal ornaments. The belts were made on a tablet loom and they were even found in Oseberg, the burial ship of a Viking queen from c. 800 C.E. The Norwegian tablet weaving technique produces a knitted look.

scarf). The scarf was a piece of white material worn to show that the wearer was married and had a certain status in the community.

A typical crown like those worn in Voss, on the West Coast, for example, measured 2½ inches high and 3½ inches at the base and a flare-out on each side of 5½ inches in diameter at the top. This style was very different from those in any other area of Norway.

> 🌸 The *lad* (a special *krone* or headdress) was decorated with metal ornaments.

As is the case of the *bunad*, each district could have a distinctive style. Crowns could be made of silver or gold. Sometimes the crowns were decorated with expensive cut jewels and oval, golden spoons, called teardrops. Sometimes the crown was heavy and had to be sewn into the bride's hair to keep it in place, and the bride's neck muscles would have to sustain the wearing of the headpiece all day long. Because crowns were expensive, they were often rented from a neighbor, goldsmith, or the church.

Kvinnebunad (woman's *bunad*) from Jølser i Sunnfjord in Sogn og Fjordane county. Another item in the bride's trousseau was a pair of fine embroidered mittens or gloves, often a gift of a young woman to her fiancé.

The bride needs the help of her mother to try on the *brudekrona* (bridal crown) that was designed at the home of Hemne i Sør-Trondalag. Lithograph made in 1852 by L. Hansen with Johan Fr. Eckersberg. Print by Chr. Tognsberg.

Carrying a Hymn Book in a *Bokformeteske*

In the 1800s it was traditional in Norway for the bride to carry her *salmebok* (hymnbook) to and from the wedding ceremony. Because the books were fragile, the bride would often carry the book in a small, chip-carved, box, sometimes called *Bibeleske* (Bible box). The box would protect the *salmebok* and make a good gift to pass on to future brides. The book itself was usually a gift from her paternal grandmother or great grandmother who probably received it at her confirmation. A traditional inscription in hymnbooks was "May you live and believe, so that you sing with the angels in eternity."

Medhus (a second home) is located in Ål, Hallingdal and was built in 1794. Rosemaling covers every available space on walls and ceilings.

A *sponeske* (a round bentwood box with slip-on cover) painted with rosemaling in late 1800s. The design is schematic but the execution is free and lively.

Bridal Boxes, *Sponeske*

Sponeske or bridal boxes varied but were usually round and measured in size from six to sixteen inches in diameter and as deep as four to eight inches. Some were large enough to carry the bridal crown or parts of the wedding *bunad*. Family or local craftsmen made the bridal boxes. Often, imported goods were not available. This meant that most items were made by hand using materials easily obtained locally, especially the bark of trees and roots of the birch tree.

The boxes were round, with bentwood sides connected by birch-root lacing, with round flat covers on top. Some boxes were made by itinerant artists going from farm to farm to sell their wares, but most such items were made by individuals on the farm. The boxes were painted mainly with rosemaling designs, using local colors similar to those of the *bunad*. Many had the date of wedding and initials of the wedding couple painted on the side or inside the box.

An oval, bentwood box with clamp-on cover was decorated by Nils Midthus in 1850, with the bride's name, Olena Olesdatter, and the date 1856 painted on the side.

The Norwegian *Tine* is a Wooden Box Used as a Wedding Gift

The *tine* was a common gift and has been given to brides for hundreds of years. The traditional Norwegian *tine* is usually a decorated, round or oval bentwood box, with handled lid, which is pressed between two upright projections. The *tine* boxes have a long history. Examples of the *tine* have been unearthed in the remains of Viking ships dating from 893 C.E. Wives went along on some Viking voyages so an item like this is not unusual. The *tine* had been used typically to store valuable personal possessions such as jewelry, needles and thread. Craftsmen carved or decorated with traditional forms of rosemaling using floral or systematically inter-related parts. Some *tine* boxes featured the date of the wedding and initials of the bridal couple.

🐾 The *tine* box was pressed between two vertical posts cut with notches. It was constructed of a piece of steam-bent wood that was laced together with birch tree root strips. They were also called snap boxes. To open the *tine*, the side posts were gently pulled apart using the flex of the wood until the lid came free and could be lifted off.

The Bridal Trunk: *Kiste*

In the countryside on farms of the 1800s, the bridal trunk was an obligatory part of weddings. Perhaps the trunk was given to the bride in childhood. In that case, the bride-to-be had her own clothes in the trunk, including everyday clothes, blankets and finery enough to last her for the rest of her life. Most likely the textiles were pieces she herself had

Hand painted trunk from Tinn, Telemark. The inscription reads: "Ole Olson Fetland Mallet (painted) Aar (year) 1868." State Historical Society of North Dakota.

spun, woven and sewn. The bridal trunk's permanent place before the marriage was in her parents' storehouse and now it would be in the storehouse of her new home. According to a firmly established tradition, the bride and trunk, among other items, were picked up the day after the wedding at her parents' home by the groom and his relatives, to be taken to the bride's new home.

Interiør fra Gulsvik, 1848. A homey farmhouse with handmade folk art. A. Tidemand.

SUMMARY

The sad part of the above story was that life was difficult in Norway for *husmenn* from the 1650s to the 1850s. Early deaths of children in the family were commonplace. Food was often scarce, depending on the weather. Snow and rain could cover the ground into spring and fall, a time when fieldwork was to be accomplished. Many crops were destroyed by unpredictable weather or disease affecting productivity. Bovine tuberculosis could not only spread from cow to cow, killing off many in the herd, but also the disease could be transferred to humans.

The happier part of the story is the importance and enjoyment the *husmenn* put on food and working with their hands. Dairy cows were the major source of rich butter and strong cheese, which were staples in daily life. Goats and cows figured prominently in the varieties of cheese production especially for *geitost,* a sweet, brown cheese made from the whey of goat's milk and cooked down and carmalized. Another favorite was *Gamalost* (lit. old cheese), a fully matured, highly pungent, sour milk cheese, light brown in color. The simple fragrances of the kitchen enriched their life and made their troubles become less of a burden. In addition, their personal folk art was many times simple or even primitive, but made with a sensitive, artistic touch. They were enriched by making useful folk pieces and, then, admiring their handcrafted bowls, knives or rosemaled cupboards. When others praised their work, they had an even deeper appreciation of the meaning of life.

The recounting of serious problems above is, indeed, a bleak summary of the life of the *husmann*, and the grasp of the total picture certainly was a good reason for leaving Norway. Nonetheless, the results of their handcrafted folk art were among the greatest output of artistic folk art the world has ever known. Their paintings, drawings and lithographs demonstrate, in great detail, their skill, craftsmanship and art.

— ENDNOTES —

1. Bjarne Hodne, Ørnulf Hodne, and Ronald Grambo. *Der stod seg et bryllup.* [We stood together in Marriage]. (Oslo: Ekteskapet i Norge gjennom tidene, 1985). pp 19-59.

2. Margaret Hayford O'Leary. *Culture and Customs of Norway.* (Santa Barbara: Greenwood, 2010). pp. 1-24. The book covers Norway in the series,

The Culture and Customs of Europe. This recent publication is valuable because it fills in the gaps in contemporary information in English on such topics as the family and marriage in Norway.

3. *National Geographic Society Traveler.* "The Fjord Region of Norway." (Washington D.C.: National Geographic Society, 1909). p. 11.

4. Veryln Klinkenborg. "Journey to the Heart of Norway." (Washington D.C: *National Geographic Society,* November, 2013). pp. 119-127. This article contains outstanding photographs of Norway's spectacular landscape.

5. Jan Sjåcik. *Historical Dictionary of Norway,* Historical Dictionaries of Europe Series. (Lanham, Maryland: The Scarecrow Press, 2008). pp. 1-19. Entries are in alphabetical order dealing with important historical figures and events, religion and the arts.

David Herlihy. *The Black Death and the Transformation of the West.* (Cambridge, Massachusetts: Harvard University Press, 1997). The book is very useful in understanding both the plague and its impact.

A carved hen was not a completely functional piece but seen as primarily a naïve rendition of birds observed in nature. A small space with a cover in the top middle was for small items like rings.

6. Janice S. Stewart. *The Folk Arts of Norway.* (New York: Dover Publications, Inc., 1953). pp. 3-26. One of the first substantive works in English on Norwegian Folk Arts, with 162 images of folk arts from all parts of Norway; 2nd edition has some colored photos.

7. Fredrick Metcalfe. *The Oxonian in Norway: Or Notes of Excursion in that Country in 1854-1855.* (London: Hurst and Black,1856). pp. 272-273. Educated and wealthy British gentlemen, many scholars at a University, would go to Norway to record folk life and then write and lecture on the subject. This section draws on Metcalfe's first-hand commentary.

Crossings: Norwegian- American Lutheranism as a Transatlantic Tradition. (Refer also to Marion John Nelson. " Folk Art and Faith Among Norwegian Americans," Todd W. Nichol, ed., (Northfield, Minnesota: Norwegian Historical Association, 2003). p. 74. Writer, Marion John Nelson, confirms the theme of this book, that folk art arose from within the rural and semi-closed societies in Norway. Nelson points this out:

> The lack of direct transfer of the tradition of folk art from Norway to America is not strange. The socioeconomic circumstances out of which that art had grown were rapidly disappearing even before mass emigration began in the mid-nineteenth century. The arts had no firm springboard from which to leap over the Atlantic. The self-sufficient economy and closed cultural units that were an important part of the context supporting folk art in Norway, never existed or were short-lived, but of a few personally motivated individuals.

Rigid heddles, were used for weaving bands, a task performed by young girls.

8. Samuel Laing. *Journal of a Residence in Norway During the Years 1834, 1835 and 1836: Made with the View to Inquire into the Moral and Political Economy of that Country and the Condition of its Inhabitants.* (London: Longman, Rees, Orme, 1836). pp. 304-360. This section draws on Metcalfe's first-hand commentary.

8a. Odell M. Bjerkness. *From Odin to Jesus: Twenty-nine Studies in Oil of Historic Stave Churches in Norway.* (Edina, Minnesota: Birchpoint Press, 2010).

9. Arizona Chapter of Norseman Federation, eds. "A traditional Norwegian Wedding." Unpublished paper is with no date or author. The writers acknowledge that the information in the paper was drawn in great part from Hodue, Hodue and Granbo *"Der Stod Seg et Bryllup."* (They Stood Together at the Wedding) (Oslo: Cappelans Forlag A.S.). This item has been helpful in providing details on rural folk weddings in the 1800s.

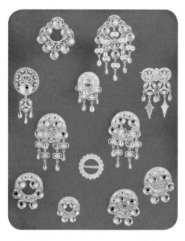

The size and decoration of the Norwegian sølje (a type of silver brooch) varies with the taste of the bride.

10. Ann Urness Gesme. *Between Rocks and Hard Places.* (Cedar Rapids, Iowa: Gesme Enterprises, 1993). pp. 91-104. Gesme wrote one of the first books in English to explain the life of the *husmann*.

11. Ingebretsen's Scandinavian Center. "Norwegian Weddings." Typed paper handout without attributions. (Minneapolis, Minnesota: Ingebretsen's, n.d.) The monograph deals with many of the details of the wedding dress. Winton Fuglie. "An 1816 Husmann's Contract." (Wadena, Minnesota: Valdres Samband, 1991).

12. Jon Leirfall. *Old Times in Norway.* (Oslo: Det Norske Samlaget, 1986). Provides colorful anecdotes and personal historical information on 1800s folk customs. pp. 76-96.
(This information came from a brochure and a personal visit to Jorvik Viking Center Museum in Coppergate, York, a tenth century Viking settlement on the east coast of England).

12a. Laing. p. 190.

13. Leirfall. pp. 77-90.

Norwegian tablet weaving produces a knitted look. These two belts date from the 1800s.

Men's folk costumes were often embellished by ornamental knives and adorned with carvings, silverwork and handsome sheaths.

14. Metcalf. pp. 221-293.

15. Leirfall. pp. 76-96.

16. Julane Lund. "The Hardanger Fiddle: The Emblem of Norwegian Identity in the U.S." (Decorah, Iowa: *Vesterheim* Vol. 7, No. 2, 2009). pp. 32-36. The article provides great detail of this unique instrument. Refer also to Alison Dwyer. "Fiddlers, Singers, and Dancers." *Vesterheim Magazine,* Vol. 4, no. 2, 2006. (Decorah, Iowa: *Vesterheim Magazine,* 2006.) p.48.

Hardanger embroidery was used around the neck of the blouse. The pin on top was a *halsnål* made in Bergen, Norway by well-known goldsmith, Peter Blytt. The lower brooch is a *glibbsølje* featuring six stylized faces.

17. Much of the information in this section derives from extensive interviews with the author's cousins, Terje and Aud Byrknes who now own the family farm, Oppegaren, on Byrknesøy. (Notes in possession of the author.) The interviews took place annually from 2005 to 2010.

18. Donald E. Gilbertson and James F. Richards, Jr. *A Treasury of Norwegian Folk Art in America.* (Osseo, Wisconsin: Tin Chicken Antiques, 1975). pp. 4-8. This is an excellent presentation of their private collections of Norwegian immigrant artifacts.

19. Paul B. Du Chaillu. *The Land of the Midnight Sun: Summer and Winter Journeys Through Sweden, Norway, Lapland and Northern Finland, Vol. 1.* (New York: Harper and Brothers, 1881). pp. 262-280. A classic example of a wealthy American going to Norway to capture in his book the life of the peasant farmers of Scandinavia.

20. Carol Hasvold works at the Versterheim Museum and wrote an article on drinking customs in Norway. sitesandstories.files.wordpress.com 2010 / dsc2739.jpg).

Embroidered mittens could be made of homespun cloth or made of knotless netting, an age-old technique dating from 300 C.E.

West Coast-style box with pull-up ends and chip carving, circa 1793. This type of box with rondels (circles) and Mickey Mouse-type ears was first seen carved at the end of Gothic church pews with a stained surface. This copy is in a small box form, belonging to the Norwegian folk tradition. The box probably was used for storing small objects like bracelets, Biblical tracts and finger rings.

We know a great deal about wedding customs in the 1800s in Norway. People in rural areas recorded their activities in personal diaries, letters, poems, songs, church records and in laws used to regulate marriage. Some common sources are British journalists and scholars who wrote about life in rural Norway from the early 1800s to the end of the century. Other sources include the Norwegian Romantic painters and lithographers, drawing their subjects from life in rural Norway.

Sociological studies, called social history in the 1800s, contributed a great deal of information. Eilert Lund Sundt (1817-1875) is considered one of the fathers of Norwegian sociology. He gathered and analyzed data, carrying out surveys and interviews in various parts of rural Norway. Some of his reports are recorded in his book, *On Marriage in Norway,* which discusses marriage at a young age, illegitimate births and night courtship (bundling) among other topics. He relates that between 1850 and 1857, his research caused him to travel continuously for 754 days. He talked to *husmenn,* laborers, teachers, civil servants, clergy and factory owners—anyone who would talk to him. His legacy is such that a building at the University of Oslo is named Eilert Sundt's Hus.]

Arizona Chapter of Norseman Federation, eds. "A Traditional Norwegian Wedding." Unpublished paper. No place, publisher or date. The paper provides many concrete examples of wedding folk traditions.

Askeland, *Jan. Adolph Tidemand og hans tid.* [Adolph Tidemand and his time] (Oslo: H. Aschehoug Co., 1991).

Bang, Marie Lødrup. Johan Christian Dahl: Life works, Vol. 3. (Oslo: Norwegian University press, 1987).

Begum, Leiv. *Sognefjorden.* (Leikanger: Skald AS, 1998).

Bjerkness, Odell M. *Images of the Valdres Valley: A Visual Tour of Norway's Historic Valdres Vallley, From the Vikings to the Present Time, Illustrated by the Author.* (Edina, Minnesota: Birchpoint Press, 2010).

Bjerkness, Odell M. *From Odin to Jesus: Twenty-nine Studies in Oil of Historic Stave Churches in Norway.* (Edina, Minnesota: Birchpoint Press, 2010).

Bjerkness, Odell M. *The Prince and the Nanny: The Life of Prince Harald, now King of Norway, as told in Historical context and through the Journal of his Nurse, Inga Berg,* (Bloomington, Minnesota: Skandisk, Inc., 2009).

Du Chaillu, Paul B. *The Land of the Midnight Sun: Summer and Winter Journeys Through Sweden, Norway, Lapland and Northern Finland. Vols. 1 and 2.* (New York: Harper and Brothers, 1881).

Eighmey, Catherine Rae. "Andrew Volstead: Prohibitions's Public Face," vol. 63 n. 8. *Minnesota History.* (St Paul, Minnesota: Minnesota Historical Society, 2013).

Eiher, Joann E., *Dress and Ethnicity.* (Oxford: Berg, 1995).

Eriksen, Thomas Hylland. *Typisk norsk: essays om kulturen i Norge.* [Essays about Culture in Norway). (Oslo: Huitfeldt, 1993).

Evensen, Knut. *Valdres: Diversity and Enchantment.* (Oslo: Boksenteret, Valdres Forlag, 1996).

Gesme, Ann Urness, *Between Rocks and Hard Places.* (Cedar Rapids, Iowa: Gesme Enterprises, 1993).

Gjermondsen, Justin. *Gar dog Bygd in Sør-Aurdal Bind B.* [Farms and Villages in South Aurdal Vol. B]. (Sør-Aurdal: Valdres Bygdesboks Forlag, 1928).

Gilbertson, Donald E. and Richards, James F. Jr. *A Treasury of Norwegian Folk Art in America.* (Osseo, Wisconsin: Tin Chicken Antiques, 1975). .

Granite Falls Tribune. Untitled news article. (Granite Falls: Granite Falls Printing, December 7, 1915). p. 1.

Hasvold, Carol. "Courtship and Marriage in Traditional Norway." *Vesterheim Magazine.* Vol. 12, no. 1, 2014. (Decorah, Iowa: Vesterheim, 2014.)

Haugen, Einar. Norwegian/English Dictionary. (Madison, Wisconsin: University of Wisconsin Press, 1967).

Helle Knut. *Gulatinget og Gulatingslova.* [*Legal assembly held at Gulen in Sogn for western Norway in Old Norse times and Gulating law*]. (Leikanger: Skald, 2001). This outstanding full-color book offers historical interpretation of the *Gulatinget.*

Hodne, Ørnulf. *Kvinne og Mann i norsk folkekultur.* (Women and Men in Norwegian Folk Culture). (Oslo: J.W. Cappelenes Forlag, 2002).

Ingbretsen's Scandinavian Center. "Norwegian Weddings." Unpublished paper. (Minneapolis, Minnesota: Ingebretsen's Center, no date).

Kleiva, Ivar. *Gulen i gammal og ny tid, Gards og attesoga, Band 3, utgave 2.* [Gulen in old and new times: Farms and people, vol. 3, 2nd printing]. (Stavanger: Verbum Grafiske, 1960). The book is a reference for people interested in finding the names of relatives and farmsteads in Gulen, Sogn og Fjordane.

Klinkenborg, Verlyn. "Journey to the Heart of Norway: Follow the Water." (Washington D.C.: National Geographic Society, November, 1913).

Laing, Samuel. *Journal of a Residence in Norway, During the Years 1834, 1835 and 1836: made with a view to inquire into the moral and political economy of that country, and the condition of its inhabitants.* (London: Longman, 1836).

Leirfall, Jon. *Old Times in Norway.* (Oslo: Det Norske Samlaget, 1986).

Liodden, Ole Jørgen. *Valdres: Norges Vakreste Eventyr. (Norway's Beautiful Story)* (Hedalen, Norway: Naturfokus, 2005).

Lund, Julane. "The Hardanger Fiddle: the Emblem of Norwegian Identity in the U.S." *Vesterheim*. (Decorah, Iowa: Vesterheim Press, Vol.7, November 2009).

Maagerø, Eva and Simonsen, Birte, eds. *Norway, Society and Culture*. 2*nd* *ed.* (Kristiansand, Portal Books, 2008). pp. 7-12. Excellent section on statistics.

Metcalfe, Frederick. *The Oxonian in Norway: or Notes of Excursions in that Country in 1854-1855*. (London: Hurst and Blackett, 1856).

Narvestad, Carl and Amy Narvestad. *Granite Falls: 1879-1979, A Century Search for Quality of Life*. (Granite Falls, Minnesota: Granite Falls Tribune, 1979).

Norlie. Olaf Morgan. *Norske Lutherske Menigheter i America: 1843-1914*. [Norwegian Lutheran Congregations in America: 1843-1914]. (Minneapolis: Augsburg Publishing House, 1918).

Norlie, Olaf Morgan. ed. *Who's Who Among Pastors in all the Norwegian Lutheran Synods of America: 1843-1924 vol 1*. (Minneapolis: Augsburg Publishing House, 1928).

O'Leary, Margaret Hayford. *Culture and Customs of Norway*. (Santa Barbara: Greenwood, 2010).

Ostlie, Wayne, Odell M. Bjerkness and Paul Ostlie. *Montevideo 1860 to 1930: Through their Eyes and in Their Words*. (Edina, Minnesota: Birchpoimt Press, 2011).

Oxaal, Astrid. *Dralt og nasjonal identitet, 1760-1917: den sivile uniformen, folkedrakten og nasjonen* [Dress and national identity 1760-1917: the civic uniform, the folk costume and the nation]. (Oslo: Doctoral thesis, University of Oslo, 2001).

Petersen, Herber. *The Great Illusion: An Informed History of Prohibition*. (New York: Gramand Press, 1968).

Sjacik, Jan. *Historical Dictionary of Norway*. (Lanham, Maryland: The Scarecrow Press, 2009).

Skavhaug, Kjersti. *Våre Vakre Bunader*. (Our Beautiful *Bunads*). (Spain: Mateu Cromo S.A, 1978).

Stewart, Linda. *Bryllup i Norge: Om bondebryllup og dagens bryllupsfeiring*. (Weddings in Norway: Farmers' Weddings and Their Day of Celebration). (Oslo: Teknnologisk Forlag, 1996).

Sundt, Eilert Lund. *Om* giftermål. *[On Marriage]*. (Christiana: Universitetsforlaget, 1867).

Takalsky, Greg. *The Anti-Saloon League and County Option: Reaching Consensus for Prohibition in Minnesota, 1879-1919*. Minnesota State University. (Mankato, Minnesota: M.A. thesis, 2005).

Wheeler, Thomas C., ed. *The Immigrant Experience: The Anguish of Becoming American*. (New York: Penguin Books, 1971).

— LOCATIONS OF FOLK MUSUEUMS —

Collections of Norwegian folk art are on display in many museums but the largest collection is in the Norwegian Folk Museum in Oslo, Norway. Almost every village in Norway has collections, either in an outdoor setting such as at Maihaugen in Lillehammer, Oppgard fylke, the Valdres Folkemuseum in Fagernes in Valdres and the Voss Museum in Voss, Sogn og Fjordane. In the U.S., the Vesterheim Museum in Decorah, Iowa has over 26,000 Norwegian artifacts in their collection.

It is helpful to understand folk art and the background of the people who created it, knowing that at the time they lived, they experienced great poverty and deprivation. As has been said many times above, many folk art experts believe that Norwegian peasants produced some of the finest and most artistic folk art created in any country.

SELECTIVE LIST OF PLACE NAMES, DESCRIPTIONS AND VOCABULARY

Most of the terms are found in the text of the book, be they place names, geographic locations, names of food or explanatory phrases.

Akevit: aquavit, liquor made from potatoes

Altar bog: Norwegian Service Book, 1889

Amerika: a word for the U.S. said with emotion, fondness and hope by Norwegians

årestua: open hearth house

Bagn: small village on Begna River where Marie Berg family lived

baroque style: characterized by ornamentation, curved rather than straight lines and by lavish ornamentation. This style of art and architecture prevailed in Europe from about 1550 to the late 1700s.

bearmann: official inviter to weddings

Begna: name of river that flows from Fillefjell in the mountains, through Bagn and running on to Lake Sperillen

beining: things people bring to weddings, be it food, gifts or money.

bjørk: birch tree, a symbol of Norwegianness

Bjørknes: William Bjørknes was a prodigious church altar painter and neighbor of Jon and Elen Byrknes

Bjørnson, Børnstjerne (1832-1910) is best known for his peasant tales such as Synnøve Sølbakken. He was awarded the Nobel Prize in Literature in 1903 and composed Norway's national anthem, *Ja, vi elsker dette landet (Yes, We Love This Country)*.

Black Death: the Bubonic Plague in 1349-1351 decimated the population of Norway.

brudefolk: bridal couple

brudeferd: a bride's journey to or from church

brudefølgje: bridal procession

brudepike: bridesmaid or flower girl

brudeseng: bridal bed

brudeslør: bridal veil

brudekrone: bridal crown or ornament worn by the bride

brunost: national brown cheese made from whey cooked down and caramelized

bryllup: has two meanings: wedding or bride's wedding dance line

bryllupsgård: the farm where the wedding is held

bunad: the Hardanger *bunad* was called the Norwegian "national" costume. The *bunad* may be seen as evidence of a group sense of identity. In Saami areas their costume, the *gakti,* dominates. Saami would wear a *bunad* only in cases of intermarriage.

Byrknes: name of the only village on Byrknesøy and means birch point or penisula

Byrknesøy: island at mouth of the Sognefjord where the Byrknes family lived

common people: were creators of the folk art of Norway as brought forth in their traditional culture, especially everyday or festive items produced or decorated by informally trained artists

Dahl, Johan Christian Clausson (1788-1857): romantic painter who focused on painting folk scenes and rural landscapes

drinking vessels: Norwegian tenant farmers carved a great variety of wooden drinking vessels—bowls, tankards and dippers, with as many variations in shapes, types of wood and different colors as there are districts in Norway

Eivindvik: largest village in Gulen and the location of the only church of Gulen in the late 1800s, where Jon Byrknes and Elen Haugen were married in 1873

filigree: delicate, lace-like ornamental work of intertwined wire of gold and silver

folk art period: Norwegian folk art covers the period from 1750s through 1850s

folk carving: dates back to pre-historical times; in the Middle Ages carvings were sometimes enhanced by adding color

folk tales: were stories of anonymous authorship and based on mythical legends handed down orally by the common people

fylke: There are three layers of government in Norway: *fylke* (county), *kommune* (municipality) and *stat* (the nation of Norway). There are other non-adminis trative terms used: *district,* used as an unofficial area organized by common language, culture, and geographical or historical background, i.e. Valdres, Gudbrandsdalen and Hallingdal. In addition, there are three church admin istrative levels: det *Folkekirken* (the folk church), formed in 2012 replacing the former state church; the *bispedømme* (diocese); *prestegjeld or menighet* (the parish) and, if there is more than one church in an area, *kirke* or *sogn.*

gård: farm

geitost: goat cheese

Granite Falls, Minnesota: Marie and Olai Bjerkness immigrated to Granite Falls and lived there for five years. Their oldest daughter, Mildred, was born there.

Grieg, Edvard, (1843-1907), Norway's greatest composer who wrote romantic folk melodies such as *Wedding Day at Troldhaugen, Hjertets Melodier* (Melodies of the Heart) and *Jeg elsker dig [deg]* (I love you)

Gude, Hans: (1825-1903) romantic painter who painted the background for Dahl's famous painting, *Brudefergen få Hardanger* (Bridal Procession on the Hardanger).

Gulen: municipality where Byrknesøy is located

Hardanger fiddle *(hardingfele)*: richly decorated Norwegian fiddle with four or five resonating strings under the four that are in contact with the bow

Haugeans: followers of Hans Nielsen Hauge (1771-1824) noted Norwegian lay preacher

Heddle: was used often for weaving decorative hair bands.

hjulmaker: wheelsmith

hulder: in folklore, the beautiful troll-girl, seducer of men, with a long cow's tail

husflid: a store where handcrafts are displayed

husmann: landless tenant farmer living in remote regions of Norway. He is a person of a lower social class, but with the special opportunity of life tenure of his rented farmland and buildings *(husmannsplass)*. This aspect of a *husmann's* contract is very special and different from any other place in Europe or Asia. In English, the word could be translated many ways: sharecropper, cotter, crofters, renters or tenants. *Husmannskone* is the wife who is also involved in working under the specifications of the contract.

Ibsen, Henrik: (1828-1906) the national playwright of Norway wrote the great folk drama *Peer Gynt,* with Edvard Grieg composing the incidental music for the play

jordkjeller: root cellar

Kerbschnitt: a common European (German) geometrical ornamentation (notch-cut pattern) that never acquired any really great importance in the mountain valleys of east Norway

Kielland (1849-1906): his most famous novel is *Garman and Worse,* a novel about the shipping industry. He was one of the "Four Greats" along with Bjørnson, Ibsen and Lie

Kingo's gradual: church altar book of 1699

kjellermann: the person who serves the drinks and uncorks kegs or bottles

kjøkemester: Master of ceremonies

klippfisk: fish dried on flat rock

klubb: potato dumplings

kommune: municipality (city, town or village)

kransekake: wreath cake made of a tapered tower of marzipan rings

kyrkje: church (modern: kirke)

laboring trades-people: folk art encompasses art produced from an indigenous culture or by peasants or other laboring trades-people. In contrast to fine art, folk art is primarily utilitarian and decorative rather than purely aesthetic.

lad: a wedding crown or headdress that is decorated with metal ornaments.

landsmaal: original name for Nynorsk

learned skills: folk artist learned skills and techniques through apprenticeships or from neighbors and family members in an informal, community setting

Lie, Jonas: (1833-1908) wrote over 30 books about the seafaring communities of north Norway

lutefisk: dried fish soaked in lye solution before cooking

mangletre (mangle board): used for ironing clothes in folk households and employed in conjunction with a long round stick

Mjømna: island opposite Byrknesøy where local church is located

Montevideo, Minnesota: Olai and Marie moved to a larger town than Granite Falls, had two more children there: Judith Marien and Odell Marvin Bjerkness. The name Montevideo comes from two Latin words *monte* and *videre,* translated, "I look around from a hill," according to Cornelious Nelson who named the town in 1870.

nisse: in folklore, small gnome-like creature

Odelsloven: right of oldest son to inherit the farm

Odin: Norse king of the gods and god of war

Oppland: fylke located in central Norway, the county where Marie Berg was born

prest: pastor

prestekrage: pastor's ruff worn around the neck

privileged position: compared to their counterparts in other European counties, Norwegian peasants enjoyed a privileged position because of their prominence in the historical development of the country and their right to rent a piece of land and buildings with tenure for life. They were never slaves.

prosperity: from 1700 to 1850 was a time during which Norwegian farmers enjoyed a certain measure of prosperity that was reflected in their rich and varied folk art, still vast poverty was evident

Queen Sonja: present queen of Norway, her daughter, Märtha Louise and daughter-in-law, Mette-Marit—all wear *bunader* at certain special events. Queen Sonja and her daughter, Märtha Louise, wear East Telemark *bunader:* Telemark is the ancestral home of Queen Sonja.

regional styles: bunader were developed and promoted in churches.

renewal of peasant art: the 1800s represent a renewal of peasant art in most parts of Norway. Peasant lifestyle changed drastically during this period with the advent of the hearth with a chimney and flue replacing the old open hearth. Other improvements included wooden floors, proper windows and large food storage cupboards.

Reinli stave church: located near Bagn i Valdres and constructed in 1300s

riksmaal: old name for Bokmaal, Dano-Norwegian

Rococo style of decoration: developed in France from the baroque period (1550-1750) characterized primarily by elaborate and profuse, often delicately executed ornamentation imitating foliage, shell work and scrolls. It was a popular design during the 18th century in churches in Norway. (cf. the Oslo *Domkirke.*).

rømmegrøt: sour cream porridge sometimes eaten with drawn butter or sugar in U.S.

rosemaling: or rose painting is decorative floral painting on walls, ceilings and furniture in rural areas, developed in the 18th century from baroque and rococo styles

rosemaling: the most recent of Norwegian peasant art was on flat surfaces

Sogn og fjordane: fylke (county) encompassing the area around Sognefjorden on west coast

Sogn og Fjordane: West Coast fylke where Olai Byrknes and his family lived in the Gulen municipality

sølje: silver brooch for *bunad* or other garments

Sør-Aurdal: municipality were Bagn is located in Valdres Valley

spillemann: fiddler at weddings

sponeske: bridal box

stabbur: storehouse on pillars as one part of farm buildings

stavkirke: stave church: medieval wooden church

Stortinget: Norwegian Parliament

syttende mai: Norway's national day (celebration of the signing of the Norwegian constitution in 1814 on May 17th in Eidsvold, Norway)

Tidemand, Adolph (1814-1876): famous Norwegian painter who worked during the 1800s in rural Norway, capturing in great detail clothing of peasants and their farms, placing examples among the finest art of the Romantic period

tine: a round or oval bentwood box with handled lid that is pressed between two upright posts or projections

tørrfisk: dried fish usually sun-dried on racks outdoors

troll: in folklore, supernatural creatures that are large, stupid and ugly

Valdres: name of an historical river valley that begins in the mountains and follows the Begna River for over 100 miles to Heddal Stave church and Lake Sperillen

Vikings: raiders, traders, and skillful seafarers from 793 to 1066

vinmonopolet: state-run liquor store

Norwegian Folk Weddings: The Norway You Never Knew is the first in a series of three related books. The second book of the trilogy is *Three Weddings and a Funeral, The Loss of Norwegian Folk Traditions*. The third volume is: *The Immigrant's Life: Contrasts in Culture*.